Contents

Microsoft®

DIGITAL
SCANNING
and PHOTOGRAPHY

DAN GOOKIN

PUBLISHED BY
Microsoft Press
A Division of Microsoft Corporation
One Microsoft Way
Redmond, Washington 98052-6399

Library of Congress Cataloging-in-Publication Data
Gookin, Dan.
    Digital Scanning and Photography / Dan Gookin.
        p. cm.
    Includes index.
    ISBN 0-7356-1012-6
    1. Photography--Digital techniques.   2. Image processsing--Digital techniques.   I. Title.

    TR267 .G66 2000
    778.3--dc21   00-036128

Printed and bound in the United States of America.

4 5 6 7 8 9   QWT   6 5 4 3 2 1

Distributed in Canada by Penguin Books Canada Limited.

A CIP catalogue record for this book is available from the British Library.

Microsoft Press books are available through booksellers and distributors worldwide. For further information about international editions, contact your local Microsoft Corporation office or contact Microsoft Press International directly at fax (425) 936-7329. Visit our Web site at www.microsoft.com/mspress. Send comments to *mspinput@microsoft.com*.

Acquisitions Editor: Christey Bahn
Project Editor: Kristen Weatherby
Technical Editor: Marc Young

Introduction

Welcome to *Digital Scanning and Photography,* your gentle, informative, and entertaining introduction to the colorful world of scanning and digital photography. Whether you currently have a scanner or digital camera, or you're peering over the graphical fence pining for one in the near the future, this book is written for you.

What You Need to Get Started

This book assumes that you're somewhat familiar with your computer and how things are connected to it, you sorta know how the operating system works, and you have an inkling about computer applications in general.

If you don't yet have a scanner or digital camera, this book teaches you everything you need to know about both, as well as general information about your computer and what's required to "do" graphics.

If you already have a scanner or digital camera, this book tells you in an expedient yet entertaining manner how each device works and how to get the most from both.

This book covers both Microsoft Windows and Apple Macintosh computers, since scanners and digital cameras can be hooked up to either. For information specific to your computer hardware, however, you'll need another reference. If you're utterly unfamiliar with the operation of a Windows computer, there are many good books at your local bookstore, including my book *PCs for Dummies.*

How This Book Works

Each chapter in this book is a complete tutorial on one specific topic of digital imaging, including how-tos on using a scanner, using a digital camera, using photo-editing software, and so on. The chapters are read front-to-back. There are various lessons within each chapter and a final Task List, which provides a quick reference for doing projects on your own.

Within each lesson are various steps to follow to accomplish some task or become familiar with some aspect of digital imaging. In some cases, I have to cover several different applications, each of which accomplishes the task in a different manner. When that happens, the steps are contained in a table. Be sure you follow the instructions specific to the application you're using.

Other Stuff You Need to Know

I've made every attempt to cover the most popular digital imaging applications, scanners, and digital cameras. Unfortunately, I didn't have room to include everything. New hardware and software constantly emerge, and there's always something someone wants to know about that's not specifically covered here.

Don't panic! Supplemental material for this book can be found on my Web page. Any updates, additions or commentary can be found at:

http://www.wambooli.com/help/imaging/

Be sure to check that page often for updates and additions to the text. And if you have any questions or would like to see something covered there that's not, you can e-mail me at dan@wambooli.com and I'll see what can be done.

Where Do You Start?

Everyone should start reading at Chapter 0, just for a quick orientation and review of where you are. Chapter 0 tells you exactly where to go and what to do next.

Enjoy your digital imaging experience!

Well, What's This?

This Chapter 0 was written to get you oriented with this book and to ensure that you get up and running with your scanner or digital camera in no time. Getting started is really not all that difficult, but using a scanner and all the graphics nonsense it involves can be intimidating. Don't fret!

Just What Is "Scanning?"

Scanning is the magic of taking an image from a photograph, magazine, book, oil painting, neighborhood manifesto, or any printed material and turning it into a graphic image you can store inside your computer. No artistic skills are required. All you need is the proper computer hardware, software and the cheerful instructions contained in this book. You'll be a scanning fool in a matter of minutes.

I got a scanner as a present and I'm eager to scan something. Where the heck do I start reading?

Chapter 3 is the place to start if you already have a scanner. Even so, I would recommend reading through Chapter 1, which discusses the computer hardware necessary to work with graphics files. Computer graphics is one area of computerdom that requires lots of horsepower. Better check your computer's stats before you dive into this.

I'm thinking of getting a scanner, am I nuts?

A scanner makes an ideal computer peripheral. Whether or not you're into computer graphics, having a scanner makes you look like a pro. Any printed image from any source can quickly be read by the scanner and transformed into a graphics file inside your computer. From there, you can use the image in a word processing document, graphics, an illustration, or a desktop publishing or Web page creation or just send the image to all your relatives in Oklahoma via e-mail.

To help you pluck out the proper scanner, Chapter 2 covers what to look for and what to avoid when scanner shopping.

Why on Earth Would Anyone Need a Digital Camera?

A digital camera works a lot like its film-based cousin. The only difference is that the pictures are stored electronically and can be instantly transferred to a computer. In a way, a digital camera is really a special type of scanner, one that's portable and hand-held and can capture three-dimensional images instead of flat images on paper.

> **NOTE**
>
> If you use a scanner primarily to scan in photographs, getting a digital camera may be a time-saving purchase.

If you don't yet have a digital camera, check out Chapter 7 for purchasing tips and other information. Chapter 8 tells you how to use the camera. Oh, and don't forget Chapter 1, which contains important information about making sure your computer system can handle a digital camera and computer graphics.

I'm Done Reading Chapter 0, Now What?

Read the rest of the book!

1 The Lowdown on Computer Graphics

Stuff Covered Here

Required computer hardware

Color printers and various papers

Graphics software

The truth is this: when you work with a scanner or digital camera, you touch down on the planet of computer graphics. Like many alien worlds, things here work differently. If you're new to the computer graphics world, then it's best to prepare yourself.

Now please don't freak out. Just about anyone can do graphics on a computer. You don't have to be a left-leaning, beret-wearing, goateed artist type. You don't need paintbrushes. You don't even need the skill to draw a stick figure. Everything is easy, thanks to your computer's graphics software. Besides, you have a scanner or digital camera to give you a decent image to start with. That's a great advantage.

On the downside, computer graphics software is demanding on your computer hardware. This chapter helps get you started by describing the requirements of graphics software, as well as how to check your computer to see if it presently meets those requirements. It's always best to start off on the right foot—or the *proper* foot if you're left-footed.

Computer Hardware Requirements

Just about any computer sold during the last five years has enough guts to run graphics software. Ideally, here's what your computer should have:

- At least 32 MB of memory (RAM)

- A high-capacity hard drive

- A fast microprocessor

If your computer has less than these requirements, you'll probably get by—though more is always better! The idea here is to make your experience with graphics applications as joyful as possible. The following sections go into additional detail.

- MB is an abbreviation for megabyte, which is one million bytes of information. Computer memory, or RAM (random access memory), is measured in megabytes.

- GB is an abbreviation for gigabyte, one billion bytes of information or 1,000 megabytes. Disk storage is measured in gigabytes.

- The microprocessor is the computer's main chip, the one responsible for making all the calculations and tossing information to and fro inside a computer. The more sophisticated the microprocessor, the easier it can handle the demands of graphics software.

You Need at Least 32 MB of RAM

Generally speaking, your computer should have at least 32 MB of RAM to work well with computer graphics files. Preferably you should have a system with 64 MB or more of RAM. If your computer has less than 32 MB, working with graphics might be slow and tedious—two words that should never be associated with using a computer.

Why All the Hardware Hoo-Hah?

The reason graphics programs demand a lot from your computer hardware is that graphics files are *humongous*! Because they contain visual information, graphics files take up a lot of disk space and memory. Plus the microprocessor has to work hard to manipulate the graphics information in memory, which is far more demanding than most other types of programs run on the typical computer.

Of course, not having a lot of hardware horsepower doesn't mean you cannot work with graphics. No, it merely means that the graphics software will run slower than it would on a computer with a faster microprocessor and more memory. For the casual computer graphic artist, that's fine; the waiting time for an image to load is often less than waiting for, say, a Web page to load. But you'll really see the difference when you work on another, faster, computer. Yowie!

Most new computers come with 32 MB or more of memory installed. Up until a few years ago, 16 MB was the standard.

Checking the RAM on a PC

To check the amount of RAM installed on a PC, follow these steps:

1. Right-click the My Computer icon.
  A shortcut menu pops up.

2. Choose Properties. The System Properties window (shown in Figure 1-1) displays your computer's installed RAM near the bottom right. In Figure 1-1, the computer has 64 MB of RAM. That's more than enough.

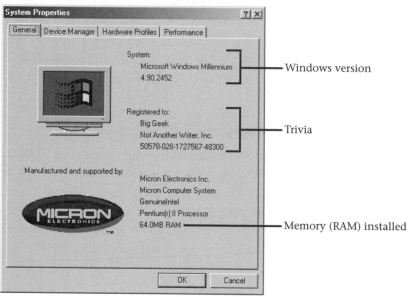

Figure 1-1. *Divulging your computer's RAM in Windows.*

3. Click OK to close the System Properties window.

Refer to the section "If Your Computer Lacks Enough RAM, Add More!" later in this chapter for information if you see something depressing, like 16 MB, listed.

Depending on your version of Microsoft Windows, the amount of RAM installed may be listed by MB (megabyte) or KB (kilobyte).

Remember that 1000 KB is the same as 1 MB.

Checking the RAM on a Macintosh

To check the amount of memory available in your Macintosh, follow these steps:

1. Choose About This Computer from the Apple menu.

About This Computer should be the first item in the menu; if not, you'll need to quit any program you're running and return to the Finder.

The About This Computer dialog box (shown in Figure 1-2) displays the amount of RAM installed in your Mac. It is the second item on the list, which is shown as 128 MB in Figure 1-2.

Figure 1-2. *The Mac coughs up its RAM values.*

2. Close the About This Computer dialog box.

Now you know how much memory is installed in your Macintosh. If you need more, you can upgrade your system as described in the next section.

If Your Computer Lacks Enough RAM, Add More!

Having enough RAM is crucial to making the graphics experience enjoyable. If your computer doesn't have the minimum 32 MB, you can always add more memory! (And adding more helps all your programs, not just the graphics applications.)

To add more RAM, I recommend consulting with your computer dealer or manufacturer. If you're comfortable with such things, you can always add more memory yourself. You should refer to your computer's technical manual for where to add the memory, how much you can add, and what type of memory to buy.

- I recommend adding as much memory as you can afford, which would prevent you from having to add more in the future. How much is enough? Oh, 64 MB or even 128 MB, or 256 MB if it's not too far out of your price range.

- The price of RAM fluctuates, with 32 MB costing anywhere from $100 to $150, possibly less depending on the marketplace.

- You can purchase RAM from your dealer or online. If you go online, I recommend Crucial Technology (*www.crucial.com*). Their online store has a nifty system for figuring out the exact RAM requirements for most computers.

You Need at Least a 2-GB Hard Drive

Graphics files devour a lot of space. A single graphics file could occupy as much as 100 MB of disk space—ten times the total storage available on the first IBM PC hard drive. To make room for not just one file but *all* the graphics files you'll eventually create, you'll need a nice, roomy hard drive.

To ensure that you have enough room for all your future graphics files, your computer's hard drive should be *at least* 2 GB in size. Ideally, a system with 8 GB or more of hard drive storage would be preferred.

(That's the typical size of a hard drive included on those new computers ideally suited for graphics.)

Checking Available Hard Drive Space in Microsoft Windows

To check your hard drive's space in Windows, follow these steps:

1. Open the My Computer icon on the desktop.

   Double-click the icon to open it. This displays a window listing all your computer's hard drives, plus a few special folders and other random items.

2. Right-click the drive C icon. A shortcut menu pops up.

3. Choose Properties from the shortcut menu.

   The drive's Properties dialog box appears. It displays information about total hard drive capacity plus a graphic representation of the used versus available space on the disk. In Figure 1-3, a 2-GB hard drive is shown with 673 MB of available space.

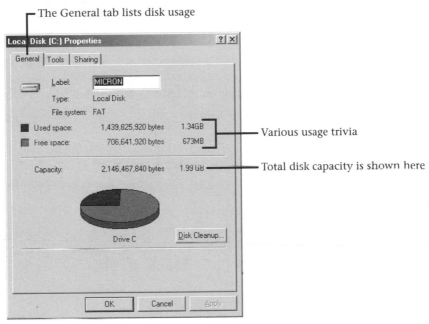

Figure 1-3. *Checking disk storage in Windows.*

4. Click OK to close the hard drive's Properties window.

The appearance of the hard drive Properties dialog box may be different depending on which version of Windows you are using. Most of them look similar to Figure 1-3 and contain the same basic information, though you may find subtle differences.

Drive C is the computer's first hard drive. It may have a name in addition to "(C:)", which is how it's displayed in the My Computer window.

Also check to see whether your computer system has drive D, which may be unused. While the C drive shown in Figure 1-3 has only 673 MB of available disk space, that system's drive D has 5 GB of disk storage available. Plenty.

There may even be a drive E available—even more storage!

NOTE

If you need more storage, add it! Refer to the section "Adding More Storage" later in this chapter.

Checking Available Hard Drive Space on a Macintosh

On a Macintosh, follow these steps to check your hard drive's capacity:

1. Click once to select your computer's hard drive.

   The hard drive's icon appears in the upper right corner of the screen in the Finder. If you can't see it, close a few windows.

2. Press ⌘+I. The ⌘I (Command+I) keyboard command is used to get information about an icon or, in the case of the hard drive, information about the hard drive. An Info window then appears, listing the drive's capacity and available space. In Figure 1-4, the hard drive holds 25.53 GB and has 24.35 GB available. Yup, you're *swimming* in storage.

3. Click the Close button in the upper left corner of the Info window to close it.

4. Click once to select an icon on the Mac. Clicking twice opens the icon.

Unless you've renamed your Mac's hard drive, it probably has the name *Macintosh HD*, where the HD stands for Hard Drive.

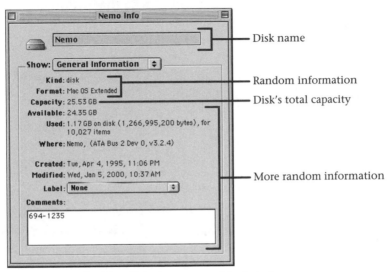

Figure 1-4. *Checking disk storage on a Macintosh.*

Adding More Storage

If your computer's disk storage is limited, you're not stuck. To supplement your computer's hard drive storage consider any of the following:

- **Get a second, high-capacity hard drive.** This is easy to add to most PCs. On Macs, external SCSI (Small Computer System Interface) or FireWire drives are easy to add, providing your computer is equipped with a FireWire port. Expect to pay anywhere from $300 to $700 for the second drive, depending on its size and whether it's internal or external.

- **Add a large format removable disk drive.** Zip drives are easy to add to any computer and Zip disks can give you anywhere from 100 MB to 250 MB of extra storage each. For even more storage, Jaz drives can be added; each Jaz disk has 1 GB or 2 GB of extra storage.

- **Add a CD-R drive.** A CD-R drive (recordable CD-ROM drive) allows you to archive or store large graphics files without taking up disk space. This isn't as good of a solution as a second hard drive or a removable drive, mostly because those drives let you expand *all* your disk storage. Still, a CD-R is a great way to store older graphics files long-term. (In the future, CD-ROM disks may supplant the family photo album!)

You Need a Fast, Fast, Fast Microprocessor

The microprocessor's speed matters, but not as much as having enough RAM or hard disk space. The speed is something that's difficult to check unless you have access to the receipt or purchase order used when you first got your computer. Your computer's microprocessor speed, measured in MHz (megahertz) is usually listed there.

Generally speaking, the larger the MHz value, the faster and better your computer's microprocessor will work with graphics.

- The microprocessor is your computer's main chip. It might also be called a CPU, for central processing unit. Microprocessors are given names such as Pentium, G4 or G3, Athlon, or other names or numbers.

- The MHz value measures the number of cycles per second at which the microprocessor thinks. It's not a fair or accurate representation of the microprocessor's true speed; the value is used for comparison only.

- Of course, speed is relative. The difference between a 550 MHz Pentium III and a 750 MHz Pentium III is only a matter of seconds when working with a large graphics file. The difference between an old Pentium 200 MHz and the 750 MHz Pentium III will be even more seconds, but still only seconds. Those seconds do add up quickly, however.

- Unlike memory and disk storage, microprocessors are something I don't recommend you upgrade. Generally speaking, it's better to buy an entire new computer as opposed to buying a mere CPU upgrade. (Buying a new computer also guarantees that you have enough RAM and a high-capacity hard drive as well.)

Finding Your Computer's Microprocessor Speed

Many PCs display their microprocessor type and speed when they first start; be quick and look in the text messages displayed on the screen. You might see "Pentium III 550MHz" displayed, and there you are!

On a Macintosh, run the Apple System Profiler, found in the Apple menu. The first panel, System Profile, lists the computer's microprocessor model name and speed in the Hardware Overview section.

Getting a Good Color Printer

The end result of most everything you create on a computer is the hard copy—the printed information. The same holds true for working with graphics; all that toil and sweat you put into touching up your images pays off once the image is permanently put down on paper. With the right printer, making the image is a snap.

Two Types of Color Ink Printers

The most popular type of computer printer sold is the color ink printer, also known as an ink jet or ink printer. These are solid, general-purpose printers, capable of high-quality color output, or they can output using only black ink when needed.

There are two types of ink printers:

- Standard, which is good for general purpose printing as well as printing in color

- Photo, which is best for producing color images and photographs

The following sections elaborate on these two types of printers.

Standard Ink Printers

The most popular type of ink printer is the standard color ink printer. This printer uses two ink cartridges. The first contains black ink, and the second contains three inks of different colors, cyan, yellow, and magenta. Because of this, these printers are known as CYMK printers, CYM for the three colors and K for black.

The three colors can be mixed in various combinations to produce an endless variety of colorful output, good for general computer use.

What About Color Laser Printers?

If you were looking for a single word to describe color laser printers, that word would be *expensive*. It just doesn't make any sense for an individual to spend all that money for a color laser printer when an ink printer or a photo ink printer will do the job.

Color laser printers are used primarily for networked groups of graphics artists who need high-speed, quality output and who have wheedled their management team into buying them such a printer.

Photo Ink Printers

Photo ink printers are designed specifically for high-quality color output. This type of printer is also known as a 6-color printer because it contains *six* color inks as opposed to the four found in a typical ink printer. More colors means that a photo ink printer can produce better output at a lower resolution than a standard ink printer. The result is better color images and extremely nice photographic reproduction.

You might see the six colors listed as "CcMmYK," which is an abbreviation for the two pairs of cyan and magenta and the yellow and black colors used. And note that some photo ink printers can be used directly with digital cameras. (See the sidebar, "Digital Camera Printers.")

On the downside, color photo printers cost more than a standard color ink printer. Also, their ink cartridges are usually a third again as expensive as the standard ink cartridges.

Digital Camera Printers

Some printers are geared to work directly with digital cameras. These printers, which usually share the same manufacturer as the digital camera, accept the camera's storage devices or memory cards directly, or they connect to the camera directly using a special cable. Connect the camera or the memory card and press a button, and the printer prints the photographs. No computer is needed!

Generally speaking, most of these printers also double as standard computer printers. Most of them are also photo printers, as described in the text.

Using the Right Paper

Printers must be fed paper. When it comes to using an ink printer, and especially if you plan on producing photograph-quality output, selecting the proper paper is key. There are four types of paper you should look into:

- **Basic copier paper.**   The least desirable choice for printing color images is plain paper or copier paper. While this type of paper works well for printing text (and it's cheap), printing color images generally results in a soaked, smeary image. I can recommend this type of paper for printing drafts; ensure that you select "draft mode" from the Print dialog box (if a draft mode is available).

- **Ink jet paper.**   Special ink jet paper is available and preferred for printing color images (and even text, if you can afford the paper). Unlike plain paper, ink jet paper really absorbs the ink well, resulting in a crisper image. The paper also has a smooth feel, which makes for very impressive documents. People love nice paper. It gets noticed.

- **Photographic paper.**   The best way to print photographs from an ink printer is using special photographic paper. This paper comes in various sizes and stocks, it absorbs ink extremely well, and it shows the image in the best possible way. On the downside, photographic paper is expensive—around a dollar a sheet. Print a few drafts on plain paper before you finalize your work on the spendy photographic paper.

FYI

Ink jet photographic paper is not the same as photographic paper you would get in a camera store. That paper is designed for use in darkrooms and creates an image using a chemical process. It should not be used in a computer printer.

- **Other papers.**   Various specialty papers exist for just about any project you can dream up. Some papers can be used to produce stickers, color transparencies, iron-on transfers, decals, and so on. They work well and can be fun. Visit an office supply store for the full collection.

Computer Graphics Software

To work with graphics files, you'll need to install some graphics software on your computer. This software not only receives the image from your scanner or digital camera, but it lets you touch up that image in various ways. The graphics software lets you perfect the image for saving to a disk or printing in much the same way as a word processor receives information from your head and lets you edit and perfect that text for eventual saving or printing.

Like many categories of computer software, graphics software covers a lot of ground. Specifically, the type of graphics application you'll be using will be "photo editing" or "image editing" software. This type of program will most likely come bundled with your scanner or digital camera, along with other graphics programs and utilities to help you work with the images you create. And if you don't like what comes with the scanner or digital camera, you can always visit the local Software-o-Rama and buy something more to your liking.

If you purchased a professional scanner or digital camera, your equipment will probably come with professional-level graphics software. If you purchased a consumer scanner or digital camera (and they say "consumer" because "unprofessional" isn't an appealing marketing term), your equipment probably came with an easy-to-use graphics application.

Using a Service Bureau for the Best Possible Output

If you want the highest possible quality output, consider a professional digital printer or service bureau.

As digital cameras become more and more popular, you'll discover that the local film processor will (eventually) accept and print your digital output. My home town has only 26,000 people, and already we have four of these places. Soon they'll be in every grocery store.

For special output, there are typically digital printing houses or service bureaus available. These places typically accept images on a Zip disk or other removable disk and let you select from a variety of output papers and sizes. A few minutes (and several dollars) later, you have a nice, crisp copy of your image.

Refer to your city's Yellow Pages under Photography or Graphic Arts for more information about these types of services.

If your equipment didn't come with a graphics application, you can always rush out to the store and buy something. Table 1-1 lists popular photo editing applications as well as other popular graphics programs.

- If you get another graphics program, ensure that it is compatible with your scanner or digital camera. Generally speaking, if the software claims to be "TWAIN compatible," it should work.

- The granddaddy of all photo editing programs is Adobe Photoshop, which defined the field when it was first introduced in the 1980s. Photoshop is a high-end, professional application, which translates as "powerful, but not too friendly."

- As an alternative to Photoshop, many scanners and digital cameras come with Adobe PhotoDeluxe. This program has many of Photoshop's features but has a much friendlier interface. I prefer it over Photoshop for simple photo editing.

Product	Description
Adobe PhotoDeluxe	The "consumer" version of Photoshop, usually bundled with low-end scanners. I've used this and can recommend it. Lots of fun.
Adobe Photoshop	*The* professional photo editing and graphical creation workshop. The learning curve on this one is a lot steeper than PhotoDeluxe, but if you're a professional or graphic artist it's a worthy program.
Corel PHOTO-PAINT	Another high-end, powerful photo editing and graphical merriment application.
Microsoft Home Publishing Suite	A package including a bevy of programs and tools for digital imaging and creating Web pages, greeting cards, calendars, and newsletters, plus tools for fixing photos and making interesting effects.
Kai's Photo Soap	A fun (I mean, software named "soap"?) image editing, cleanup, and simple effects application. Photo Soap is wonderful for fixing up old photographs, removing red-eye, and creating general glee.

Table 1-1. *Graphics software worth a look.*   *(continued)*

Table 1-1. *continued*

Product	Description
Kai's Super Goo	A program used to create goofy photo effects. (They use the word "goofy" in the product description.) I've seen this product bundled with several scanners, along with other image editing software.
Microsoft PhotoDraw 2000	Microsoft's own graphical workshop, replete with powerful graphics imaging and editing tools. This product is available with the Microsoft Office 2000 Premium suite or can be purchased separately.
Microsoft Picture It! 2000	A wonderful photo editing, printing, and digital image management program. I know quite a few digital camera users who can't live without it.

Task List

1. Check how much memory is installed in your computer.

   To guarantee that your computer graphics experience is a pleasant one, you should ensure that your computer's hardware has what it takes to keep the computer graphics software happy. That means at least 32 MB of RAM.

2. Check how much disk storage your computer has.

   There should be at minimum 2 GB total. The more, the merrier. Don't forget about the D drive on your PC (if you have one). And a good way to add more storage is by purchasing a removable disk drive or CD-R.

3. Get a good color printer.

   If you don't yet have a printer, consider getting a photo printer. Otherwise, any standard ink printer should do you well.

4. Buy some nice paper.

   Get some of that wonderful ink printer paper for high-quality output. And if you really want to impress people, get some photographic paper.

5. Get graphics software.

This may not be necessary, providing that some graphics software comes with your scanner or digital camera. And if you don't have a scanner or a digital camera to complete the picture, refer to Chapter 2 for scanner shopping and Chapter 7 for information on choosing a digital camera.

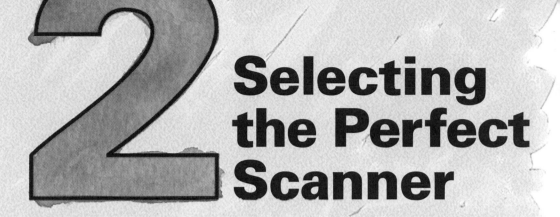

2 Selecting the Perfect Scanner

Stuff Covered Here

Items that affect a scanner's price

Things to look for in a scanner

An assortment of scanners, from cheap to lavish

Computer scanners were once rather exotic things. If you found one at all, it was in a graphic arts shop. I remember first playing with a scanner back in 1988 in the production department of the magazine I worked for. It was slow, it could only scan in black and white, and it was expensive.

Thanks to advancing technology and dropping prices, scanners today are as common as keyboards. They're fun and useful, and make a great gift (along with this book). If you don't yet have a scanner, this chapter shows you the ropes on how to get one. If you already own a scanner, consider this a quick review of your scanner's basic abilities.

The Bottom Line: Price

If you're cheap, you don't need to feel guilty about buying the cheapest scanner. Oh, if there's a brand name you like or maybe the picture on the box intrigues you, that's okay. But generally speaking, just about any scanner will do the job. Buy a cheap one.

Okay. So you're not convinced. Maybe you want to know a little bit more about scanners and, for example, why there is a difference between a $69 scanner and one costing $399—or even $2499! Yes, they all do the same thing, but there are definite reasons why some cost more than others. Most of those reasons are related to the following basic scanner attributes:

- Resolution

- Color depth

- Optical density

- Interface

There are other scanner attributes that affect price as well, including the scanner's size, speed, bundled software, options, and other technical mumbo jumbo. These items are covered later in this chapter.

Like the price, the technical description of a scanner's ability will probably be right there on the scanner's box. Items such as resolution, color depth, optical density, and so on should all be listed. If you're buying online, the items should be listed on the Web page. Otherwise, you can phone the scanner manufacturer for all the details.

Resolution: The Higher the Better (but Not Too High)

The main reason for one scanner being more or less expensive than another is the scanner's *resolution*. That's a gauge of how much information (detail) the scanner can read from an image. The higher the resolution, the sharper the image. (See Figure 2-1.) And with that higher resolution comes a higher cost.

Six dots per inch   24 dots per inch   A zillion dots per inch

Figure 2-1. *Various scales of dots per inch.*

The scanner's resolution is measured in dots per inch (dpi). Values range from 300 dpi on up to 2400 dpi or even higher. That tells you how many pieces of an image the scanner can read on a horizontal line. The more dots per inch the scanner can read, the more detail you will have in the final image. A "consumer" or low-end scanner might have a resolution of 300 dpi. That's just fine for the home, for saving pictures to the Web, or for having fun.

Mid-range scanners for business or general purpose might have a resolution of 400 to 600 dpi. This higher resolution makes the scanner ideal for office-related graphics work and reproducing or touching up photographs.

High-end, professional scanners have a minimum resolution of 600 dpi and go up to 1200 or 2400 dpi. This high resolution (at least 1200) is required for working with color slides or film negatives. If you're not planning on doing that type of scanning, you don't need to pay the extra money for such a high-resolution scanner.

The thing that determines a scanner's resolution is the *image sensor*, which is covered later in this chapter.

If you plan on using your scanner for Optical Character Recognition (OCR), you don't need more than 400-dpi resolution. (OCR is where the scanner is used to read a document and save its contents as a text file.)

Refer to Chapter 5 for information on monitor, printer, and scanner resolutions.

There Is a Difference Between "Optical" and "Interpolated" Resolutions!

Most scanners actually have *two* different resolutions, and scanner manufacturers often list the higher resolution on the box—without telling you which resolution it is. This can be sneaky.

The first type of resolution is *optical* resolution. That's the number of dots per inch the scanner reads using the image sensor (the device that actually scans the image—more on that later in this chapter).

The second type of resolution is *interpolated*, also known as Maximum Interpolated Resolution (MIR). This is a higher dpi value than the optical resolution, made so by using software to help boost the numbers. The software "guesses" higher resolution values and produces an image at that higher resolution. It's like magic!

Between the two, always use the optical resolution when scanner shopping. The manufacturer can "play" with interpolated resolutions, but optical resolutions are fairly solid things and a better gauge of a scanner's abilities.

Now, there's nothing wrong with an interpolated resolution. For example, if you have a scanner with a 300-dpi optical resolution, it might be capable of a 1200-dpi interpolated resolution (and it will say so on the box). That's fine for basic graphics work and producing images for the Web. It's *not* fine for scanning color negatives, which need at least 1200-dpi *optical* resolution.

All the resolutions listed in the section "Resolution: The Higher the Better (but Not Too High)" are optical resolutions.

How Deep Runs the Color?

Walking hand-in-hand with the scanner's resolution is the color depth value. This value is measured in bits, and it determines how many levels of color the scanner can capture. In a nutshell: the higher the bit value, the better the scanner is able to discern between two subtly different shades of the same color. This is a plus.

The minimum color depth on a typical scanner should be 24 bits. Avoid 8-bit scanners, which barely produce the variety of colors necessary to let you adequately reproduce a photograph. (Too low of a color depth value can result in "noise," which is incorrect or, let's face it, *ugly* colors around the midtones in an image. Tacky. Tacky. Tacky.)

Color depths of 30 to 36 bits are best, with 36 bits being the bestest. You absolutely need 36 bits if you plan on scanning color slides or negatives.

A bit is a binary digit, or a number that can be either one or zero. Though that may seem insignificant, when you group bits into clumps of 24, 30, or 36, they can represent millions of values.

Don't worry about your printer having a lower color depth value than your scanner. You always want to scan an image at the highest resolution and color depth, regardless of the resolution or color depth of the output device. Having more information than you need is always a plus.

On Top of the Optical Density

Closely linked to the color bit depth is a scanner's optical density (OD). Unlike other values, the optical density might not be listed on the side of a scanner's box, though the value is important. What it gauges are brightness values in an image, with higher OD values being better than low values.

Most scanners have an optical density of 2.8 OD to 3.0 OD. This is fine for most uses. If you plan on scanning color slides, you need a scanner with an optical density of at least 3.2 OD. If you're scanning color film negatives, you need a scanner with an optical density of about 3.4 OD. And it goes without saying that these higher OD values add to the scanner's cost. (Of course, if you plan on scanning color slides or film negatives, you should plan on paying more for a scanner anyway.)

- It's the scanner's image sensor that determines the optical density. See the section, "The Almighty Image Sensor" later in this chapter for the technical details.

- OD values may also be listed as D (without the O). Don't let that throw you.

Finding the Proper Interface

The final basic determination of a scanner's price has nothing to do with the scanner's ability to scan images. No, the final determination is how the scanner connects to your computer—its *interface*. There are three common interfaces, and a fourth, newer interface, the FireWire standard, which you'll most likely see more of in the coming years. But first, the basics:

- **Printer port.** The most basic scanner interface is the PC's printer port. This is an ideal, low-end solution since the great majority of PCs come with printer ports. On the downside, there are other devices that attempt to use the printer port as well (such as external disk drives). This leads to printer port hogging, which is messy and involves endless cable swapping. Because of that, the printer port connection is my least favorite choice for connecting a scanner.

- The PC's printer port is also known as a *parallel port* or *parallel interface*.

- If all you have connected to your PC's printer port is a printer, selecting a printer port scanner is fine. If you already have devices other than the printer connected to the printer port, another type of scanner interface might work better for you. My advice: Consider upgrading your PC with a USB expansion card.

- **USB.** The basic interface standard of the Macintosh, the Universal Serial Bus (USB) allows you to easily connect a scanner to any iMac, Power Macintosh, or even a PC with a USB port. (I've used the same USB scanner on both a PC and a Mac.) The only true downside to the USB interface is that only newer computers tend to have USB ports. Then again, it's easy to add a USB interface to any computer by plugging in a USB expansion card.

- **SCSI.** Currently the best scanner interface is SCSI (Small Computer System Interface), which is pronounced "scuzzy." This interface is common on older Macintoshes and a few high-end PCs, though you can add a SCSI expansion card to just about any computer. The SCSI interface allows you to connect a variety of devices, including all types of disk drives, tape backups, and, of course, scanners.

    SCSI scanners are usually high end, high resolution, high color depth, high OD, and other high and mighty things. The only downsides are that not every computer is equipped with a SCSI interface, and dealing with SCSI devices can be frustrating and time-consuming.

TIP

Avoid scanners that use their own SCSI or proprietary interface. You will never get the same performance from that interface as you will from a bona fide, real SCSI interface. I recommend upgrading your system with a nice, fast, high-end SCSI interface if you plan on using a SCSI scanner.

- **The future? Firewire!** Better than SCSI for high-end scanners is the FireWire interface. FireWire offers the flexibility and ease of use of USB with speeds faster than SCSI. As this book goes to press, there are few FireWire scanners available. In the future, however, most mid-range and high-end scanners will use the FireWire interface.

Other Things to Look for in a Scanner

Less important than resolution, color depth, optical density, or the interface are the more esoteric and technical aspects of a scanner. Here's the list:

- Size
- Speed
- Bundled software
- Image sensor
- Special options

These all affect price, but more important than that is just knowing what they are and how they affect the scanner's performance.

Scanner Size and Type

The scanner's size isn't really its physical dimensions but rather the size of the glassy area where the image is placed. For most scanners, it's the size of a sheet of paper or slightly larger. You pay more for a scanner that can handle a larger image, say legal size or larger.

The primary type of scanner available today is the flatbed scanner, which looks like a squatty photocopier. A few years ago there were hand-held scanners that worked like tiny vacuum cleaners you swiped over an image. These were a cheap alternative to the then-expensive flatbed models. (With today's lower prices, such a cheap alternative is no longer necessary.)

Out on the fringe, you may find some specialty scanners. I've seen tiny business card scanners. There are special scanners that only scan in color slides. There is also a highly portable hand-held scanner, more commonly known as a *digital camera*. See Chapter 7 for more information on digital cameras.

Scanner Speed

Some scanners may tout how fast they can acquire an image, but like any speed test, the values are meaningless because they can be manipulated in the lab. In real life, *everything* takes time to accomplish.

If you're in a hurry, you can pay more and get ultra fast scanners, but speed should never be a shopping issue. Instead, the issue here is to avoid multipass scanners. These scanners actually scan an image three times, once for each of the basic colors (magenta, cyan, and yellow). Nearly all of today's scanners are single-pass, reading the image in one swipe. Avoid anything else.

Software That Comes with the Thing

The scanner should come with basic software. The more you pay for the scanner, the more and higher quality the software that comes with it. Here's a breakdown of the software normally included with a scanner:

- **Drivers.** This is the software required to run the scanner—basic operating system programs.

- **Scanning Program.**   This is the program that operates the scanner, adjusting its many options and actually acquiring the image. The scanning program doesn't run by itself, but is instead used by image-editing software or other software to acquire the image.

- **Image or Photo Editing.**   All scanners should come with basic image-editing software. If you pay more, you might get advanced image-editing software, such as Adobe Photoshop and maybe other photo-editing applications. (See Table 1-1 on page 19.)

- **OCR software.**   This type of software is required to read documents, scan the text, and create a text file on the computer. Some low-end scanners may not include OCR software.

- **Other software.**   There's a whole mystery grab bag of software that might come with your scanner. The scanner's manufacturer tosses this stuff in to add "value" to the scanner and to entice you to buy. Who knows what it could all be? Generally speaking, the more you pay for the scanner, the more software gets tossed in.

TIP

Don't feel pressured to install everything at once; you can get by with the drivers and image editing software to start. Install the additional software later as you learn what you really need. For example, I rarely install the OCR software included with a scanner because I don't need it.

The Almighty Image Sensor

The image sensor is the official doohickey inside the scanner that reads the image being scanned and turns it into bits for the computer's digestion. There are two types, CCD and CIS.

- **The CCD image sensor.**   The better of the two types of image sensor is the Charge-Coupled Device, or CCD. This device is generally capable of higher resolution than the CIS type of image sensor (see next page). However, the CCD requires more electronics to do its job, which means a scanner with this type of image sensor is more expensive.

- **The CIS image sensor.** This is the more common type of image sensor, found mostly in smaller, lighter scanners. CIS stands for Contact Image Sensor. It is also called a CMOS Image Sensor.

Which is best? It depends. Resolution and color depth are more important than the type of image sensor. Whether the manufacturer chooses one or the other doesn't matter as much as the basic scanner attributes covered in the first part of this chapter.

Other Options and Stuff

The most common scanner option is a transparency adapter, which allows you to place a color slide or film negative into the scanner. This device is necessary because the scanner's light must *shine through* a transparency and not be reflected off of it. So if you plan on scanning slides you need a transparency adapter—in addition to the resolution and optical density requirements that type of scanning demands.

TIP

Be sure to check the size of the transparency adapter, should you need one. Some are small, designed for color slides or 35mm negatives. If you plan on scanning larger transparencies, you'll need a larger adapter.

Another option is the automatic document feeder, which is used primarily with OCR software in business applications. This device is singularly responsible for skyrocketing a scanner's price into the thousands of dollars. An automatic document feeder shoves paper into the scanner the way paper is fed into a printer or fax machine. Some of these document feeders have the ability to shove upwards of 80 pages per minutes into the scanner. Of course, at that price, the scanner can actually read the images that quickly. Wow.

Transparency adapters might be called a TPA or TPU. I've no idea what these acronyms stand for, though they're commonly used.

Scanners with automatic document feeders also come with document management software.

  Digital Scanning and Photography

The Gamut of Scanners, Cheap to Oh-My-Gosh!

How much will you pay? That all depends. Table 2-1 lists what I feel are the four basic categories of scanner, with their prices and various technical aspects. The terms "Low-end," "General," and so on are my descriptions. When shopping, you should use the cost as the basis of which category a scanner fits into.

	Cost	Resolution	Comments
Low-end	Under $100	300 dpi	Home use, Internet
General	$100 to $300	400 to 600 dpi	Usually includes bundled applications
Mid-range	$300 to $800	600 dpi or more	Higher-end bundled applications. Might also include a transparency adapter
High-end	$800 and up	1200 dpi or more	High OD, advanced software, maybe a sheet feeder

Table 2-1. *Gauging scanners by their type, price, and options.*

All scanners typically have a bit depth of 30 to 36 bits, though the low-end scanners may have only 24 bits—which is fine for that level of scanner. Higher bit depths add to the cost, but also increase the quality of the images you scan.

If you're worried about getting stuck with a cheapy scanner, go for the "General" type ($100 to $300 in price), which should suit you well. The price fluctuates based on the resolution, interface, manufacturer, and any bundled software.

Remember, at the higher prices, you're paying for a more advanced image sensor and higher optical density. That technology is really needed only for scanning color slides, transparencies, or film negatives.

Task List

1. Review your scanner needs.

   The best way to buy anything is to first figure out how you're going to use it (now or in the future). If all you're doing is scanning pictures and images for the Internet, save yourself some money and get a low-end scanner. If you want to do a little more with graphics, consider a higher-end model.

2. Research some scanners on the Internet.

If you have an Internet connection, visit an on-line computer store where you can shop for scanners. Scanners are usually their own category or can be found under "hardware" or often "input devices." Notice the scanner's prices and how the price affects the resolution, bit depth, and interface as covered in this chapter. Find the most expensive scanner available and determine why it costs so darn much!

3. If you don't have a scanner, buy one.

Review the technical specifics of what you need:

- Resolution

- Bit depth

- Optical density (a high value is required only for scanning slides or negatives)

- Interface

Now plunk down your money and proudly march back to your computer with its new toy.

3 Introducing Your Scanner

Stuff Covered Here

Unpacking and setting up the scanner

Identifying basic scanner parts

Connecting the scanner and installing software

Welcome to Scanner 101, your basic computer scanner introduction and orientation course. Please, please, hold all your questions until the end of the chapter. This is basic stuff, but worthy of a review even if you're impatient and ready to scan something (which comes in Chapter 4).

It's assumed you already have a scanner and are ready to become familiar with it and even install it if you haven't already done so. If not, refer to Chapter 2 for information on buying a scanner.

Unpack Your Scanner!

If you've just purchased a scanner or received one as a gift, open it up! Take it out of the box. Remove the foam packing material, plastic wrapping, and any tape. Locate the cables, manual, software, and other documentation, and put them aside.

Set the scanner on your desktop where you imagine it will finally go. If this requires that you shove some papers, books, and junk out of the way, so be it! Remember that you need access to the scanner by opening its top lid, so don't set it anywhere that's too confining.

The scanner can be as far away from the computer console as the cable will stretch, but you'll probably want to keep it close.

Don't connect or install anything yet. Next comes some orientation and identification.

- Try not to set stuff on top the scanner. I know this is hard. And stacking manuals, books, or the laundry on top of the scanner will eventually happen. Even so, remember you need to lift the scanner's lid to use it, so treat the top of the scanner as a sacred place. (There's nothing physically wrong with setting stuff on the scanner, it's just inconvenient.)

- I would keep the scanner's box for about a month or so, just in case the scanner proves defective and you need to return it. After a month, feel free to throw the box away or recycle it.

- Keep the manuals, disks, and other materials in a safe place. I have one shelf in my office for the associated manuals, disks, and documentation that go with my computer.

Basic Scanner Parts

Scanners are rather basic devices. They have fewer buttons or knobs than your printer or monitor, and the only part you can move is the lid. There is one on/off button. One light. And there are two cables, one for power and the other connecting the scanner to the computer. That's basically it, but an illustration always helps.

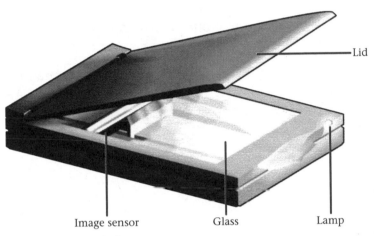

Lid

Image sensor   Glass   Lamp

Figure 3-1. *A typical scanner.*

Figure 3-1 shows a typical scanner, probably quite similar to the one on your desktop. In addition to the scanner itself, locate the other items mentioned in the list. You should be familiar with the following:

- **The lid.** The lid swings up to accommodate whatever you're scanning. Note that the lid is flexible in the back—maybe even removable—to allow you to scan images from thick books or magazines. Yes, it's just like using a copy machine.

- **The glass.** The glass is where you place the image to be scanned, face down. Around the glass, you'll find tick marks, similar to a copy machine. These tell you where to place the paper and help you line up images. (It's best to scan an image as squarely as possible.)

- **The sacred image sensor.** Visible through the glass, nestled inside the scanner, is the eye that scans the image. It's a long, thin device that usually contains some form of fluorescent lamp. The image sensor slides down the length of the scanner to read the image. You might also be able to see some electronics beneath the image sensor in the back of the scanner. Oooo!

- **Slide adapter.** If you have a scanner capable of scanning 35mm slides, color negatives, or similar transparencies, the adapter, tray, slot, or doohickey will appear somewhere on the scanner. (There is no standard look or location for it, so I left it out of the illustration.)

- **The power lamp.** This is the light that comes on when you turn on the scanner. The light may blink when the scanner is in operation, or it may flash rapidly to indicate various errors. Some scanners may have more than one lamp, in which case they will be labeled, "power," "error," and so on.

Figure 3-2 shows the exciting rear end of the typical scanner, the end that faces away from you. The things on the scanner's rear are important, but you'll probably visit there only once during the scanner's setup. The list:

- **Power switch.** The scanner's on/off button. You can turn the scanner off when you're not using it. Some scanners have a "sleep mode" that automatically shuts the scanner off after a period of boredom.

TIP

Some scanners may have no on/off button at all! No problem: the scanner will turn itself off after a period of inactivity. If you ever need to turn the scanner on and off (such as when the computer has trouble finding it), you'll need to unplug it, wait, then plug it in again.

- **Power cable connector.** This plugs into the wall.

- **Computer cable connector.** This plugs into the computer. The cable should come with the scanner. Don't plug this in just yet! Wait for the hardware installation section later in this chapter.

  Digital Scanning and Photography

- **Optional connectors.** The scanner may have a connector to attach optional devices, such as a transparency adapter. Scanners that use the PC's printer port will have a "pass through" connector to which you attach the printer's cable. And SCSI scanners might have a second SCSI connector to attach additional SCSI devices.

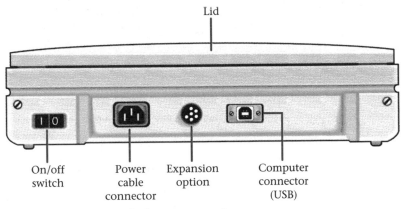

Figure 3-2. *Things to find on a scanner's rump.*

Don't Forget to Unlock the Scanner!

A feature in some scanners (and an extra button, to boot) is a locking mechanism. This is used to prevent the image sensor from sliding around during shipping; however, you must unlock the scanner before you can start using it.

Don't forget to unlock the scanner!

If your scanner has a lock, you should be able to locate it on the top near the back. The switch should be labeled with "lock" and "unlock" or the appropriate international symbols. The scanner must be unlocked before it can be operated.

If you plan on shipping the scanner again, then lock it. Otherwise, you don't need to lock the scanner, even if you're just moving it to another table. And don't be disappointed if your scanner doesn't have a lock. Not all of them do.

Installing the Scanner Software

Your computer, being a rather shy device, must be formally introduced to your new scanner. You do this by installing proper scanner software for the computer to use. This has to be done for every computer.

Before installing the software, an important note: Some scanners insist that you must connect the scanner to the computer before you install the software. Other scanners must have the software installed before you connect the hardware. Hardware first? Software first? Refer to your scanner's manual for the proper sequence of events.

NOTE

All scanners should come with software. If you haven't found the software, search the scanner box again.

Insert the scanner software disk into your computer's CD-ROM or DVD drive and follow the instructions on the screen or printed in the manual. (Each installation is subtly different depending on your scanner and your computer.) I can offer you the following tidbits of advice:

- Generally speaking, select whichever installation option is prechosen for you, the standard, typical, easy, or "default" option. That should set everything up nicely.

- If you're given a choice, try to install only the software you'll need right away. That includes the scanner's drivers or initialization programs plus the image editing software. You don't need to install *everything*. If you're unsure about installing something, then don't.

- When the installation software asks that you quit all other programs, it's merely being safe. Generally, most installation programs require you to restart your computer after they run. If you quit other programs, your important data files and documents are all safely saved to disk. You can restart without the fear of losing anything.

Connecting the Scanner to Your Computer

This is super easy, thanks to the fact that there's not really much to plug into the computer when you have a scanner.

Plug In the Power Cable

All scanners require electrical juice to operate. Ensure that the scanner is turned off, and then plug one end of the power cord into the scanner and the other end into a wall socket or power strip.

There is no need to plug your scanner into an Uninterruptible Power Supply (UPS). Those battery-backed power sources are best used for temporary power to the computer and monitor in case of a power outage. Plugging a scanner into a UPS would be a waste; scanning can take place *after* the power comes back on.

Using the PC Printer Port Connection

To connect the scanner to your PC's printer port, follow these steps:

1. Turn off the computer and printer.

2. Unplug the printer from the computer. Note where you unplug the printer. That's your PC's printer port. Remember its location.

> **TIP**
>
> There is no need to unplug the printer cable from the printer itself; keep that end plugged in.

The printer will plug into the scanner instead of plugging directly into the computer. Yes, this sounds weird, but it works. See the sidebar, "Beware the Printer Port Daisy Chain!" for more information.

3. Connect the scanner to the computer. Plug the scanner's cable into the printer port on the back of the computer. Plug the other end of the cable into the proper connector on the back of the scanner. It might be labeled "To computer," "Data in," or something similar.

4. Connect the printer to the scanner. Take the loose end of the printer's cable (the one you unplugged from the computer) and plug it into the back of the scanner. Figure 3-3 illustrates the final configuration.

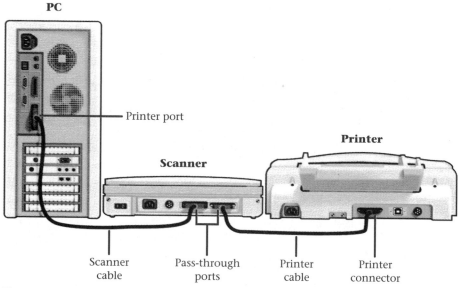

Figure 3-3. *Connecting a scanner to a PC via the printer port.*

Check for loose ends, and if everything looks well and good, you're done! If you haven't yet installed the scanner's software, do so now.

If your PC doesn't have a printer, you can just connect the scanner directly to the computer's printer port.

The PC's printer port must be configured to both send and receive information, which is called *bi-directional* mode. If the scanner requires any other mode, it should say so in the manual. Your PC's setup program lets you change the printer port mode. (It's different for every computer, so you'll have to refer to the computer's manual for the details on using the setup program.)

If you experience problems printing, it might be because the scanner is turned off. Otherwise, the printer should operate normally. (There may be a notice in the scanner's manual that says you shouldn't print while scanning.)

Beware the Printer Port Daisy Chain!

The printer port is a great place to quickly and painlessly add new hardware to your computer. In addition to scanners, you can also add external disk drives, Zip or Jaz drives, CD-ROM, CD-R, CD-RW, and DVD drives using your PC's printer port. This is all fine, and the printer will still work normally, but you shouldn't add more than one device between the computer and printer.

Problems happen when you try to "daisy chain" several devices on the printer port. For example, you cannot connect your scanner and then a DVD drive and *then* the printer to the printer port. This puts too many demands on the printer port, which was really designed only for use with a printer and not as a method of hardware expansion. (The fact that you can add a scanner or disk drive using the printer port is merely a bonus.)

If you're desperate to have more than one device attached to your computer's printer port, you can try connecting them both to an A-B Switch. This may or may not work with all printer port devices. A better solution, of course, would be to forget about the printer port and upgrade your PC with a USB or FireWire port instead.

Connecting a Scanner to a USB or FireWire Port

Adding a scanner to your computer's USB or FireWire port is a snap—literally!

- Plug one end of the cable into your computer and the other end into the scanner.

Voilà! That's it. Both USB and FireWire ports work the same. Just plug the thing in, and you're ready to go.

The USB cable should come with the scanner. It's an A-B cable, which means it has one flat end (A) and a larger, truncated-square end (B). The flat end plugs into the computer, and the square end plugs into the scanner.

If your computer has a USB hub, you can also plug the scanner into it—one of the virtues of USB.

USB scanners don't need to be connected to the computer at all times. Just connect the scanner whenever you plan on using it. Otherwise, you can store the scanner elsewhere.

Wrestling with the SCSI Connection

SCSI is the most contentious type of scanner connection, but on the upside, it's also one of the fastest. Some industry pundits claim that SCSI is the inspiration behind the simple and versatile USB and FireWire ports. Whatever.

If at all possible, I would recommend having someone else set up and configure the SCSI part of your scanner. Of course, if you have SCSI and are used to it, the following steps might make sense to you. If not, have someone else do this.

1. Obtain a SCSI ID for the scanner.

2. Plug the scanner into a SCSI port.

3. Ensure that the SCSI devices are properly terminated.

Sounds easy, of course. And some SCSI adapters are easier to work with than others. Fortunately, this needs to be done only once.

Always ensure that the scanner has its own ID, one not used by any other SCSI device.

If your scanner has a fixed ID, you might need to change the ID of another SCSI device in your system. For example, if the scanner must be set to ID 6 but you have a tape backup drive at that address, change the ID of the tape backup. Do this before installing the scanner. Restart the computer to ensure that everything works.

Beware of "self-terminating" devices! These SCSI devices supposedly save you time by removing the termination requirement (another bane of SCSI). However, self-terminating devices must be the last device in the SCSI chain. If you already have a self-terminating device, just put the scanner between that device and the computer.

Another common problem can happen if you use improperly designed SCSI cable converters. Some SCSI devices use a small cable; others use a large cable. To switch between them, you need to buy a high-quality cable converter. Cheapie converters will cause you nothing but headaches! (I recommend the Adaptec converters.)

Your SCSI scanner should be turned on before you turn on the computer console. If you don't do this, the scanner may not be recognized or "found" when you need to scan something.

Turn the Thing On!

Ta-da! It works.

The scanner should power itself up, hum, make some adjustments, and blink its light. This is all normal. If it doesn't appear normal, refer to your scanner's manual for soothing words of advice.

You're now ready to scan, which is covered in the next chapter.

The biggest source of scanner start-up woe is not unlocking the image sensor! Make sure that thing is unlocked before you turn on the scanner.

If you're using a SCSI scanner, run your computer's SCSI utility to confirm that the scanner has been recognized.

Task List

1. Confirm all the parts of your scanner.

Use the information in Figures 3-1 and 3-2 to identify every part of your scanner. If there's something odd on your scanner, refer to the manual for information on what it could be. Don't try to pick anything off your scanner unless you know what it does.

2. Connect your scanner, and install the software.

Remember to check the manual to determine whether the scanner needs to be connected first or the software needs to be installed first. Knowing this ahead of time saves you a ton of hassles.

3. Make sure the scanner is operating properly.

A scanner operating normally doesn't do anything when it's on and ready to work. The light shouldn't be blinking. Confirm with the manual if you see anything unusual, such as a blinking light or an annoying grinding sound from within the scanner.

  Digital Scanning and Photography

4 Scanning and Saving an Image

Stuff covered here

Running the imaging and scanning programs

Previewing and selecting the image

Saving the image in a specific graphics file format

The reason for having a scanner is to scan. It's the main point, the big deal, *el grandé enchilada*. But scanning itself plays only a small role in the big picture. Almost as important as scanning is saving the image to disk. After all, there is no single graphics file format. There's GIF, TIFF, JPEG, and on and on. You need to choose the proper format depending on where the image ends up. Don't panic! Whatever the case, this chapter shows you how to get from here to there in a friendly and informative manner.

There are perhaps a dozen common graphics file formats. The uncommon and unique file formats number in the hundreds.

The GIF, TIFF, and JPEG formats are explained later in this chapter.

Start by Running Your Imaging Software

The first step to using a scanner is to run the software that will receive the image, what I call "imaging software." It could be the program that came with your scanner, such as Adobe PhotoDeluxe or Adobe Photoshop LE, or it could be other graphics or imaging software that promises to work with a scanner.

Start that program now!

If you've turned your scanner off, turn it on now.

Likewise, if you've disconnected a USB or FireWire scanner, re-attach it before you run the imaging software.

Imaging software could also be called photo editing software. It can be any graphics application on your computer, but it *must* be one that lets you use your scanner to acquire an image.

Next, Run the Scanning Program

The imaging program does not itself scan the image. Instead, you need to run another program, one that controls the scanner. I call this program the *scanning program*. It lets you preview the image, select the part of the image you want to scan, and then send the image back into the imaging program.

The imaging program launches the scanning program. You select a special menu command or click a button on a toolbar. Then the scanning program takes over, allowing you to work the scanner.

The scanning program you use will have its own unique name. For example, the scan program used by the Umax line of scanners is called VistaScan. That's the example used in this book. The scanning program you have might look different but will have similar controls.

(Yes, this is strange. If it all made perfect sense, this book wouldn't be necessary.)

Activating the Scanning Program

Running the scanning program is done differently depending on your imaging software. Many of them work similarly, using the same or similar menus or toolbar buttons. Remember that you must have already started the imaging software before you can run the scanning program.

The methods for activating the scanning program for popular applications are listed in the table below.

Application	Method for Activating
Imaging for Windows	1. On the File menu, click Scan New. 2. Choose your scanner from the Scanner menu. 3. Click the Scan button.
Adobe PhotoDeluxe (Windows)	1. Click the Get Photo button. 2. Click the Get Photo tab. 3. Click the Scanner button's drop-down list. 4. Choose your scanner from the list, and click OK.
Adobe PhotoDeluxe (Mac)	1. Click On Your Own. 2. Click Get Photo. 3. Click the Scan Photo button. 4. Choose the scanner from the Available pop-up list, and click OK.

Table 4-1. *Commands for activating the scanning program in popular imaging applications.* *(continued)*

Table 4-1. *(continued)*

Application	Method for Activating
Photoshop/LE	1. On the File menu, click Import. 2. Choose your scanner from the Import submenu. (If your scanner isn't listed, then you need to select it using the TWAIN Select submenu.)

Note that graphics applications use special verbs to refer to "getting the image from the scanner." In some applications the word is *acquire*. Other applications may use the word *import*. The command is generally found in the File menu.

Where Did the Scanner Run Off To?

Sometimes your imaging software may report that the scanner cannot be found. Yes, even though it's sitting right there, the software just can't seem to locate the scanner. This happens every so often to just about everyone.

The first thing to check is the scanner's connections. Is the scanner plugged in? Is it connected to the computer? Is the scanner turned on? Some USB scanners may "hang" and require you to reconnect them or turn them off and then on again. Some computers might not recognize a scanner unless it is turned on when you turn the computer on.

If you consider all of these questions and options when you're faced with a stubborn scanner, you should be able to get the thing working again in no time.

Beginner or Advanced Mode?

Many scanning programs have two modes, one for beginners and another for advanced users. The only difference is that the beginner mode lists the most popular selections for you. In the advanced mode you must set these options manually. Figures 4-1 and 4-2 illustrate the differences.

Image preview

Switch to advanced mode

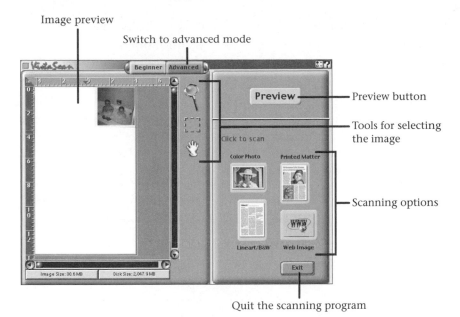

Preview button

Tools for selecting the image

Scanning options

Quit the scanning program

Figure 4-1. *A scanning program's beginner mode.*

Image preview

Switch to beginner mode

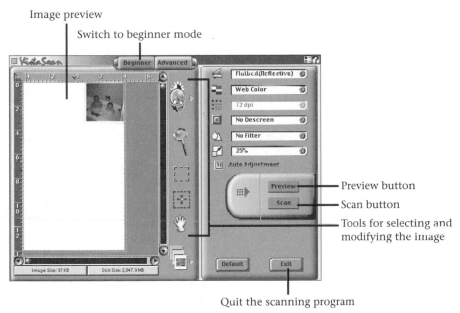

Preview button

Scan button

Tools for selecting and modifying the image

Quit the scanning program

Figure 4-2. *A scanning program's advanced mode.*

For now, stick with the beginner mode. Not all the tools are available in the beginner mode, but for most scanning operations the tools listed should get the job done. Keep in mind that beginner mode is not "baby mode." It just lists the most popular selections in an easy-to-use fashion. If there is no beginner mode, then just use whichever options are already set. You will learn more about the options available in advanced mode in the next chapter.

Looking Over the Scanning Program

The scanning program you see on your screen may look different from the ones shown in Figures 4-1 and 4-2, but the basics are still there. Your scanning program may or may not have all of the following:

- The image preview area, where the image to be scanned appears

- A Preview button

- Tools for selecting the image

- Options for adjusting the image, usually visible only in the advanced mode

- A Scan button or similar buttons for scanning the image

- An Exit or Cancel button

Note that the Scan button may be disguised in beginner mode. It may appear as a number of choices, as shown in Figure 4-1. Also be aware that some scanning programs have both a Scan *and* OK button. The OK button typically means you're done with scanning and want to quit.

FYI

You may already see something in the preview image area of the scanning program. That's merely the "leftovers" of what you previously scanned. Nothing to worry about.

Load the Original

Place the thing you want to scan face down into your scanner. This original can be anything you can press down on the scanner's glass. Try to find something colorful and interesting for your first attempt.

Please: for the purposes of this exercise, do not attempt to scan your face.

Important Information About Copyrights

Yes, you can scan anything. If it fits into the scanner, you can make a copy. Electronically, there is no problem. Legally, however, there might be a problem.

Unless you created it yourself, most things you might want to copy are protected by a copyright. Under United States Copyright Law and most international treaties, a copyright owner has the exclusive right to control reproduction, distribution, and modification of their copyrighted material. If you're not the original creator or owner of the image you want to scan, forget it! I encourage you to contact the copyright owner directly for any necessary permission or license, but they'll probably say "no."

But don't get discouraged yet! The Copyright Act provides for *fair use* of a copyrighted work for purposes such as criticism, comment, news reporting, teaching (including multiple copies for classroom use), scholarship, or research. This means you can use portions of a copyrighted work in your projects, but you should consider the following:

- What's the purpose of your project? Is it for commercial gain or a nonprofit, educational purpose?

- How much of the copyrighted original are you using? Consider the size of the portion you're copying in relation to the size of the entire document.

- What's the effect of the use upon the potential market for or value of a copyrighted work, if any?

For comprehensive information regarding copyright law, you can check out the many available resources on copyright law on the Internet or in your local library, or—if you're really bored—you can contact an attorney.

As you're facing the scanner, the back part (the part farthest from you) is the "top." Place the top side of the image you're scanning back there (face down, remember). Otherwise the image you scan will be upside down—which is fixable, but it's always best to do things right the first time.

Be sure to note the tick marks along the edge of the glass. That will help you line up an image. There may be one specific triangle in the corner or center of the back part of the glass. That tells you where to specifically line up images for the best possible scan.

If you need to, you can remove the scanner's cover to scan extra thick material. Like a copier, the cover is not required for scanning, but should be replaced after you're done scanning.

Previewing the Image

Your first duty in the scanning program is to preview the image you're scanning. Unless you tell it otherwise, the scanner scans the *entire* glass area. While that's keen and all, it's usually more than you need. By previewing, the scanning program allows you to select only that part of the image you need to scan.

- Click the Preview button.

    The scanner may calibrate itself. It's adjusting the image sensor. You may hear humming or clicking. Wait.

    The scanner lights up like a photocopier as the image sensor scans the entire glass inside the scanner. This takes a few seconds. If you have a multi-pass scanner, then the image sensor may make several sweeps.

    Eventually the image appears in the preview window. In Figures 4-1 and 4-2, you can see the old photograph I scanned in the upper-right corner of the preview window. Note that the scanner previews the entire glass area, even though the thing you want to scan may only occupy a small portion of that area. So the next step is to select only that area for scanning.

Now you can start to see why previewing is necessary; not every image you scan will fill the entire glass or be in the same position on the glass for scanning.

Selecting and Cropping

After previewing the image, you need to select the portion of it you want to scan. This is done using the lasso tool.

If the image is small, you can use the magnifying tool to enlarge the image in the preview window.

Magnifying your Image

1. Click the magnifying tool to select it.

2. Click the part of the image you want to enlarge to magnify it.

Part of the preview screen gets bigger. If you need to zoom in more, click again.

3. To zoom out, press and hold the Alt key on your keyboard while you click (use the Option key on a Macintosh).

This changes the plus sign (+) in the magnifying tool to a minus sign (–), which means you're zooming out instead of in each time you click. (If that doesn't work, refer to the scanning program's manual for proper zoom-out instructions.)

Now you're ready to select the portion of the image you want to scan.

Selecting your Image

1. Click to select the lasso tool.

The lasso tool back in Figure 4-2 looks like a square with dashed lines. It may appear differently in your scanning program, though it does the same thing.

2. Click the upper-left part of the image and drag the lasso tool down and to the right to "box in" the portion of the image you want to select.

As you position the mouse over the image, note how it changes to a cross-hair pointer. When you release the mouse button, that part of the image is selected. A line of "marching ants" may appear around the selection. Figure 4-3 shows how this all works.

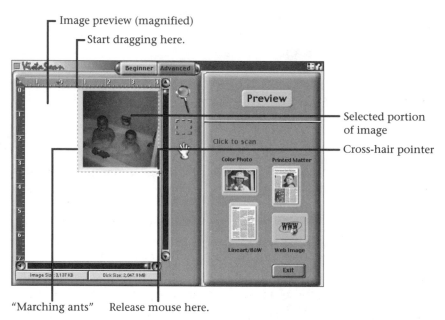

Figure 4-3. *Using the lasso tool to select part of the image.*

TIP

Don't fret over being exact! You can always crop and fix your image in the imaging software. If you can't get the lasso exactly where you want it, select more of the image than you need. Imaging software has more powerful tools for fixing an image than the scanning program does.

With a portion of the image selected, you're ready to scan.

Digital Scanning and Photography

- The area selected by the lasso tool can be adjusted. Just click the edge or corner of the selection and drag in or out to change the selection size.

- The hand tool can be used to move the selection without resizing it.

- If you cannot resize the selection, it's probably because you're using the magnifying glass or some other tool instead of the lasso tool. Click on the lasso tool to reselect it, then resize the selection.

- Of course, different tools may be available in different scanning programs. Feel free to experiment with these tools if you wish. Nothing is scanned until you click the Scan button.

Scan!

This is easy:

- Click the Scan button

    If your scanning program lacks a Scan button, then there's probably another button used to scan. For example, the VistaScan program shown in Figure 4-1 uses the four buttons (Color Photo, Printed Matter, Lineart/B&W, and Web Image), each of which is a Scan button. You click the button that best represents the type of image you're scanning, or if you're scanning something for the Internet, you click the Web Image button.

    Scanning may take a while, in which case there might be some sort of entertaining graphics on the screen to amuse you while you wait.

    La-di-da. . .

    When the scanning is done, the image is placed inside your imaging software. You're now done with the scanning program and can close it. In some cases you may need to click the OK button to close the scanning program.

Holy Moses! That's Huge!

Don't be surprised to find that the image you scanned is, well, *humongous* on the screen. If it doesn't appear overly big, two things are possible. The graphics program could be showing you the image "zoomed out." If, so you can find a proper Zoom command to display the image at 100% of its true size. (Yup, it's big.) Or, you could have scanned it in as a Web image. That image has the same resolution as your computer's monitor, but the image will lack the detail of the other options.

The reason the image is so big has to do with the *resolution*, specifically the difference between the scanning resolution and the resolution of your computer's monitor. I'll discuss this relationship more in the next chapter.

- A zoom size indicator is usually shown somewhere in the program, either on the image window's title bar or on a toolbar. Try setting the image to 100% to see how big it looks.

- Some images are displayed large on the screen but actually print out smaller. This has to do with the scanner's resolution, which you can adjust (as shown in Chapter 5).

- Chapter 5 also discusses how to resize the image to something more reasonable.

Saving in the Proper Format

After scanning, the image is placed into your imaging software. A good thing to do at this point is save the image to disk. Saving something to a disk is a simple operation for most of the programs you use. You select a folder for the file, bless the file with a name, then click the Save button, and the file is safely stored. Oh, sometimes you may have to worry about saving it in this or that format, but most of the time you name the file, save, and you're done. Not so with graphics applications!

Most graphics applications let you save an image in a variety of formats. Why? It depends where the image ends up; some formats are better than others. Here's the short list of image file formats:

- The "native tongue" format

- GIF

- JPEG

- TIFF

First among the formats is the graphics program's native tongue. For example, Photoshop saves its images in the Photoshop format, Microsoft PhotoDraw saves its images in PhotoDraw format, and so on. Each unique format is best for use in its application. If you open up a Photoshop document in Photoshop, then it's just the way Photoshop wants it. There is no importing, conversion, or loss of information. (As an example, Microsoft Word's native format is the document, or "doc." That's better for use in Word than, say, a plain text file, though the plain text file contains the same words.)

The other formats, GIF, JPEG, and TIFF, are what I called the "shared" formats. These formats can be read by a wide variety of applications, and they each have their own, best purpose.

GIF and JPEG formats are best for Internet images. Both formats have a perfect resolution for e-mail or a Web page, and they consume little disk space. GIF is better for artwork and detailed images; JPEG is better for photographs.

The TIFF format is best for sharing images with other applications. For example, not every application may be able to understand a Photoshop image but most applications—including your word processor or spreadsheet—know what a TIFF graphics file is.

There are even more graphics file formats available for other, specific needs. Appendix B lists them all, though for the most part you'll be using native tongue, GIF, JPEG, or TIFF.

More information about GIF, JPEG, and TIFF

GIF stands for Graphics Interchange Format. It's pronounced either *giff* or *jiff*, and sometimes both ways if you can't agree on either one. The GIF file format stores images in smaller files, but with good detail. It's a common format for images on the Internet.

JPEG (or JPG) is another Internet graphics file format. It stands for Joint Photographic Experts Group. You pronounce it "jay peg" whether it's spelled JPEG or JPG. This graphics file format is even smaller than GIF, but not as detailed. For photographic images—faces, landscapes, people, scenery—it's preferred. Most of the images you scan for the Internet should be saved as JPEG. Only if the image looks blurry or cheap do you need to bother with the GIF format.

TIFF stands for Tagged Image File Format. Say, "tiff." This graphics format is the Esperanto of graphics files. Just about every program that works with graphics (even word processors) can consume a TIFF file, which stores lots of good graphical information. On the downside, TIFF files are huge; a single TIFF file can be many megabytes in size. This is why they're best suited for exchanging graphics files between applications and not well suited for the Internet.

Saving the Graphics Image in the Native Format

After editing the image (if necessary), you're ready to save it to a disk. Saving in the graphics application's native format allows you to re-edit the image later. Saving in another format may not save the unique information used by the program, so having a copy in the native format is a good idea.

Saving your Image

1. Click Save on the File menu.

The Save dialog box appears, shown in Figures 4-4 and 4-5. Remember that not every application uses the same Save dialog box. They're similar, but not truly identical.

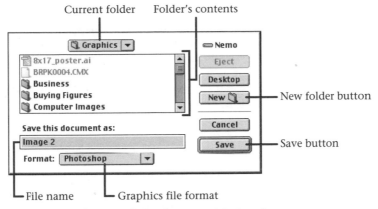

Figure 4-4. *The Save dialog box on a Macintosh.*

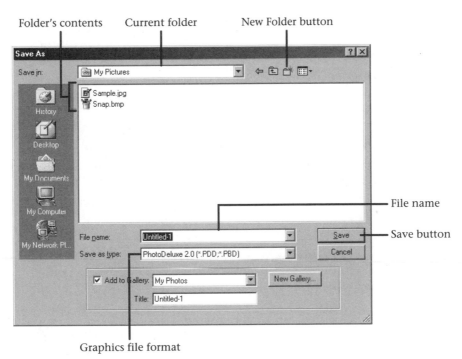

Figure 4-5. *The Save dialog box in Windows.*

2. Choose a location for the file.

Use the dialog box's tools to find a disk drive or folder for the file. If you don't have a special folder, use the new folder button to create one. It's best to keep all your graphics images in one place, or at least a folder with other related files.

If you're using Windows, look for the My Pictures folder and store your images there. You can create a My Pictures folder if you don't have one. And you can even create folders within the My Pictures folder to keep your graphic images organized.

IMPORTANT

Do not save your graphics files to a floppy disk. If you want to save graphics files to a removable disk, use a Zip disk or CD instead. Floppy disks do not have the capacity to store graphics files.

3. Give the file a name

    Short and to-the-point names are best.

4. Choose the file's format

    The graphics file format list (see Figures 4-4 and 4-5) lets you save the image in a variety of formats. With some graphics applications, a format other than the program's native format may be selected. If so, change that item back to your graphics application's native format. (You'll be saving in a special format in the next section.)

5. Click the Save button

    This saves the file to disk, but in some cases another dialog box may appear allowing you to set additional options. If so, click OK in that dialog box to continue saving the file to disk.

    The image is now safely saved on disk, but in the graphics program's native format. To save in a specific format, continue reading with the next section.

FYI

You don't always have to save in the native format. For this tutorial, it's OK. But if you know you're creating JPEG images for the Internet, then saving a native tongue copy is unnecessary and wastes disk space.

  Digital Scanning and Photography

Saving in the JPEG, TIFF, or Other Formats

Saving in a non-native format requires you to take some extra steps, primarily to choose another graphics format depending on where the image will end up. This is unusual for most applications, though it's common to save word-processing documents in plain text format. In graphics applications, the ability to save in multiple formats is actually a feature of the software.

There are two ways to save in a non-native image format: by using the Save As command or by using a special Export command. It works differently for each program, the most popular of which are listed in Table 4-2.

Application	Method for Saving
Adobe PhotoDeluxe (Windows)	1. On the File menu, click Send To. 2. To save the file as a JPEG, choose File Formats. 3. Use the file format drop-down list in the Save As dialog box to save the image in any of a number of formats. 4. Click the Save button. 5. Make additional adjustments or just click OK in any further dialog boxes that appear.
Adobe PhotoDeluxe (Mac)	1. On the File menu, point to Export, and click File Formats. 2. Use the file format pop-up list at the bottom of the Save dialog box to choose the JPEG, TIFF, or other file format. 3. Click the Save button. 4. Click OK in any supplemental dialog boxes that appear (allowing you to customize the image format).
Photoshop/LE	1. On the File menu, click Save As. 2. Choose a graphics file format using the format types list at the bottom of the Save As dialog box. 3. Click the Save button. 4. Click OK in any additional dialog boxes displayed.

Table 4-2. *Commands for saving an image in JPEG, TIFF, or other formats.*

Additional dialog boxes may appear for the JPEG or TIFF file formats that allow you to set other options. For the most part, clicking OK in these dialog boxes is the best option.

- Alas, there appears to be no TIFF export command in PhotoDeluxe for Windows. (Better upgrade to Photoshop.)

- Yes, it would make sense if all the file formats were merely on the same standard Save dialog box. (I hope someone from Adobe reads this.)

Saving in the GIF Format

Saving in the GIF format is done differently than saving in the other (JPEG, TIFF) formats. Table 4-3 illustrates the commands needed to save in the GIF format for three popular imaging programs.

Application	Method for Saving
Adobe PhotoDeluxe (Windows)	1. On the File menu, click Send To. 2. To save the file as a GIF image, choose GIF89a Export. 3. Click OK, and then use the Save dialog box to save the image.
Adobe PhotoDeluxe (Mac)	1. On the File menu, click Export 2. To save the file as a GIF image, choose GIF89a Export.
Photoshop/LE	1. On the File menu, point to Export and click GIF89a Export

Table 4-3. *Commands for saving an image in the GIF file format.*

What's the fuss with GIF formats?

The GIF format is actually owned by CompuServe (which is owned by AOL). To use the format, the graphics application developer has to pay a licensing fee. This is probably the reason why the GIF export command is often kept in a different place from the other exporting commands. I assume if someday CompuServe were to revoke the GIF license, having a separate menu would make it easier to remove the GIF option from the program. But that's only a guess.

Quitting Your Imaging Software

When you're done scanning and saving for the day, you need to quit your imaging software. This isn't a big deal, though occasionally, when you quit you may see a "You haven't saved this document to disk" type of dialog box. A puzzling look may cross your face . . .

When you export an image in a non-native file format, the application program (rather rudely) assumes that you really haven't saved the file. Even though a TIFF or JPEG or GIF image may exist on your computer's hard drive, you still haven't saved the image in its native tongue. The application lets you know this by displaying a warning.

Do you need to always save in the native tongue? No. If you've already saved or exported the image in another format, then you're OK. Click whichever option tells the program not to save the image—that it's OK to quit—and be on your merry way.

Task List

1. Scan an image and save in the native format.

    Find a picture and scan it in to your graphics program. Run the scanning software to acquire the image. Preview and crop the image. Scan. Save the image to a disk using your graphics application's native format.

2. Scan an image, and save it as a JPEG file.

    Remember that JPEG images are small in size and best suited for photographs. So dig up a photograph and scan it. Save the image as a JPEG.

3. Scan an image, and save it as a TIFF file.

    After saving the image, quit your graphics application and open your word processor. Use the word processor's graphics commands to open the TIFF image and place it into your document. (You don't have to save this, just do it once to prove that it works.)

5 How Resolution Works

Dealing with computer graphics becomes a lot easier when you understand the holy concept of *resolution*. It plays an important role in determining image quality, so choosing the proper resolution is key to scanning, editing, and finally getting the printed result just the way you want.

This chapter covers resolution and how it impacts the images you scan, edit, and print. Also covered is the sacred topic of color depth and how that fits into the big picture.

Why Is Resolution Such a Big Deal?

Resolution plays a big role in computer graphics. Bottom line: it's the resolution that determines how *good* the image looks. This would lead you to logically pronounce, "Then I must use the *highest* resolution possible to ensure that all my stuff looks so very, very good." Alas, such logic just doesn't hold water when it comes to computer graphics.

Instead of striving for the highest resolution you should try for the *best* resolution. Sure, a resolution of a gazillion pixels per inch would be impressive. But consider the following points: Can the scanner scan such an image? How long would it take? Would such an image tax your computer hardware to sluggish immobility? And even if you could work at such a high resolution, what about the printer? Could the printer output at that high resolution? Would it all be truly necessary? Just because you can do such a thing never implies that you need to.

FYI

Choose a resolution based on what you plan on doing with the image. Keep in mind that there is no magic formula for choosing a resolution, no handy rules, cheat sheet, or tables to follow. The best way to determine a proper resolution is through experimentation and, honestly, what looks good. The resolution values suggested in this chapter are for reference only.

Instead of the highest, strive for the *best*. This chapter shows you how to do just that. When you choose the best resolution, you're using your computer, scanner, and printer combined to help you create the image you need. You don't want to bite off more pixels than you need, but on the other hand, you want enough pixels to produce a quality image. That's what choosing the proper resolution is all about.

Everything Has a Resolution

Alas, graphics resolution isn't a single topic. Sure, all resolution is generally measured in dots per inch (dpi). But with computer graphics there are three resolutions you need to concern yourself with:

- The image's resolution

- The monitor's resolution

- The printer's resolution

Each of these plays a role in the images you create and manipulate. Each has its own resolution, which can often be set higher or lower depending on your needs. The following sections cover each item's resolution and how you can adjust it to get the images you want.

The Start of It All: Image Resolution

The image's resolution determines how much detail is present in the image itself. The higher the resolution, the more detail available, which makes for easier image editing as well as nicer reproduction when the image is printed.

If you're using a digital camera, the camera sets the image's resolution when you snap the picture. With a scanner, the scanning software sets the resolution. The minimum and maximum resolution values are determined by the digital camera or scanner, and the image is then created using the number of dots per inch you specify.

As an example, suppose you're scanning in an old photograph—one of those 4-inch-by-4-inch color pictures popular in the 1960s and early 70s. (See Figure 5-1.) You choose to scan it at 600 dpi. That's a mid-range resolution value for most scanners, a value that should provide plenty of detail if you plan on editing the image. (If that isn't enough detail for you, then you can always rescan the image at a higher resolution.)

4 inches
x 600 dpi
―――――――
= 2400 dots

4 inches
x 600 dpi
―――――――
= 2400 dots

5,760,000 dots in all

Figure 5-1. *A 4-inch-by-4-inch image at 600 dpi.*

The actual amount of detail provided by 600 dpi is trivial; you don't need to know it every time you scan, since you'll be using your eyeballs and the image editing software to perform the actual work. If you really must know, the detail can be determined by doing some simple math.

At 4 inches times 600 dots per inch, you get: 4 × 600 = 2400. This means there are 2400 dots horizontally and another 2400 dots vertically in the image. That translates into a grid of 2400 × 2400 = 5,760,000, or nearly six million dots or individual blips of information that compose the picture. This tells you how many color dots the image has, but the actual value isn't something you need to know when you work with graphics. In fact, the only thing it really tells you is approximately how huge the image file will be on disk.

At 600 dpi there will be lots of dots, which translates into plenty of information for you to be able to edit and eventually print the image.

Digital Scanning and Photography

But say you were scanning in an image for the Web. In that case, you can get by with a resolution of, say, 150 dpi. Why? Because computer monitors typically have a resolution of 72 or 96 dpi. Information created for the Internet need only work with such low resolutions, so the "best" resolution in this case is something close to 72 or 96 dpi.

For trivial purposes, here's the math for an image scanned at 72 dpi (such as that in Figure 5-2): 72 dpi by 4 inches equals 288 dots horizontally by 288 dots vertically. That's a grid of 82,944 dots. It's a lot less than the detail you get for a photo scanned at 600 dpi, but for the Web that's all you need. (Remember, you don't have to make this calculation when you scan an image; I'm just using the math to illustrate how much information is available in the image.)

4 inches
x 72 dpi

= 288 dots

82,944 dots in all

Figure 5-2. *A 4-by-4 image at 72 dpi.*

The image is always the same size no matter what resolution you scan it in at. A 4-by-4-inch image is still 4 inches square whether it's scanned at 25 dpi, 150 dpi, 400 dpi, 1200 dpi, or higher. It's only the resolution—the detail *in* the image—that changes.

The higher the resolution, the longer it takes to scan the image. It's the price you pay for packing so much information into the digital image. Likewise, images with very high resolutions severely tax the computer's resources, making even the fastest PC or Macintosh slow to a crawl. It's an ugly trade-off, but sometimes necessary.

How Much Resolution Is Enough?

Calculating image resolution isn't always necessary, but it does help you to understand how much information is carried in a higher resolution image. But you still may be asking, "How can I tell how much resolution is enough?" The answer is determined by two things.

First, the image's resolution depends on how much information you need to edit the image. If you plan on blacking out teeth or adding a moustache, a lower resolution would be fine. But if you plan on doing some detailed editing, such as fixing scratches in the photograph, a higher resolution is required. In those circumstances more information is always best, so push the resolution to the wall.

The second factor is the resolution of the output device, the printer. All printers only have so much resolution. You must take that into consideration when you scan in an image, and also if you plan on enlarging the image. All this is covered in the section "Finally, It's the Printer's Resolution," later in this chapter.

Then There's the Monitor's Resolution

All monitors have a resolution, which is usually given in horizontal by vertical pixels. For example, a popular monitor resolution is 800 x 600 pixels. That's 800 pixels across by 600 pixels down, which displays a goodly chunk of information on the screen.

A monitor with a 1024 x 768 resolution displays more information than one with an 800 x 600 resolution. However, at a higher resolution, the icons and other images on the screen appear smaller. The icons aren't really smaller, it's just that the same number of pixels used to create an icon (32 pixels tall by 32 pixels wide) appears smaller when the monitor resolution is higher. This is why the monitor's resolution isn't popularly described as a dots-per-inch value, as image resolution is; as the monitor's resolution changes, the dpi value changes. That can get confusing, which is the reason monitors are normally gauged in straight horizontal-vertical resolution values.

FYI

High resolutions generally demand a larger monitor. For example, a 17-inch monitor may be able to support the 1024 x 768 resolution, but things will look better on a 19-inch or 21-inch monitor. (And if you plan on working with graphics full-time, a large screen monitor is a must.)

Your computer monitor's resolution can be changed using the computer's operating system. Most people set it to something comfortable to view, though when working with graphics software, it helps to set the monitor to the highest resolution possible. That way you can see more of your image on the screen at once.

Setting the Monitor's Resolution in Windows

The Display Properties dialog box controls many monitor settings in Windows. You access this dialog box through the Display icon in Control Panel:

1. On the Start menu, point to Settings, and click Control Panel.

Display

2. Double-click the Display icon to open it.

3. Click the Settings tab to display that part of the dialog box (shown in Figure 5-3).

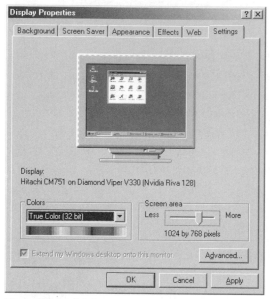

Figure 5-3. *Setting the monitor's resolution in Windows.*

Use the options on the Settings tab in the Display Properties dialog box to set the monitor's resolution and color depth. The Screen Area part of the dialog box lets you set the resolution higher or lower. The corresponding size of the images on the screen is shown in the preview window. Click OK to confirm the settings, then follow the instructions on the screen to view the new resolution.

Setting the Monitor's Resolution on a Macintosh

The quick and dirty way to set the monitor's resolution on the Mac is to use the Control Strip—that triangle thing hugging the left or right side of the screen. Click it to make it slide out, and then click the Monitor Resolution button (shown in Figure 5-4) to see a pop-up list of resolutions. Choose your new resolution from that list.

Figure 5-4. *Click the Monitor Resolution button on the Control Strip to change resolutions.*

Digital Scanning and Photography

Another way to set the monitor's resolution is to use the Monitors control panel. From the Apple menu, choose Control Panels, and then click Monitors (or Monitors & Sound). This displays a dialog box similar to the one shown in Figure 5-5 where you can set the monitor's resolution as well as color depth (discussed later in this chapter). Choose the resolution from the displayed list; close the dialog box when you're done.

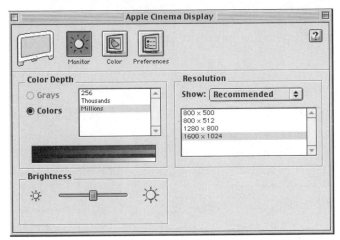

Figure 5-5. *Set the monitor's resolution in this dialog box.*

How Does the Monitor's Resolution Play a Role?

Your monitor doesn't affect an image's resolution at all, but it does affect how that image appears on the screen. You can test this using your own computer's monitor.

1. Scan an image at 100 dpi.

    Scan the image at 100 dpi using your scanning program. You may have to switch to Advanced mode to set the resolution to 100 dpi. Save the image to disk, giving it a name like 100DPI or whatever lets you know the image was scanned at 100 dpi.

2. Rescan the same image at 800 dpi.

    Save the image to disk with a name such as 800DPI.

    You may have noticed that the 800 dpi image appears much larger on your monitor than the 100 dpi version. That's because the monitor shows the same number of dots (pixels) per inch for each image, so it would make sense that an image at 800 dpi would appear "larger" since the monitor's resolution doesn't change.

    There's nothing that can be done about this weird resolution relationship. Yet, software developers are aware of the problem and include in their imaging applications a Zoom command for enlarging or reducing the image displayed on your screen. The Zoom command can be found in a menu or on a floating palette or toolbar, or can be accessed from the keyboard.

3. Use the imaging software's Zoom command to display the 800 dpi image at 100 percent.

    Big, huh?

4. Use the imaging software's Zoom command to display the 100 dpi image at 100 percent.

    (You may have to close the 800 dpi image to open the 100 dpi image.) The 100 dpi image should look more or less "normal" in size. Why? Because its resolution is closer to your monitor's resolution. That's all!

    By using the Zoom tool, you can enlarge a specific area of an image for editing. This is where a high monitor resolution truly pays off; when you zoom in on a high-resolution image, you'll find lots of information to play with. Zooming in on a low-resolution image reveals large clunky squares of color. Figure 5-6 illustrates this concept, with a high resolution image on the left and a lower resolution image on the right.

Zoom into 800 dpi scan Zoom into 72 dpi scan

Figure 5-6. *Zooming into a high-resolution and low-resolution image.*

Other handy tools for working with images include the Fit-In-Window, Actual Size, or Actual Pixels commands, usually found in the imaging software's View or Window menu. You can use these commands as instant ways to zoom or reduce an image you're working on.

Digital Scanning and Photography

Finally, It's the Printer's Resolution

If the image will eventually be printed, then choosing a proper resolution mostly depends on the output resolution of your printer. At first guess, it would seem proper to scan in the image at the same resolution as the printer. For example, it seems logical that a 600 dpi printer would make a lovely copy of a 600 dpi image. But that's not really the case.

You always want to scan in the image at a *higher* resolution than the output device. So if you have a 600 dpi printer, then scanning the image at a resolution higher than 600 dpi would be best. More information is good, remember? So scanning at 800 dpi would result in better output. If you can handle the longer time it takes to scan and work with the image, then doubling the resolution to 1200 dpi would be jolly good.

You should also consider the printer's resolution if you plan on enlarging the image. For example, suppose you plan on enlarging a 4-by-6 photograph to an 8-by-10 print. If so, you'll need more information in that scanned image to make the larger version look good.

Beware of choosing too high a resolution! Suppose the printer has a resolution of 600 dpi. That means an 8-by-10 photograph could have a resolution of 4800 horizontal by 6000 vertical dots. Scanning in an image at 2400 dpi might work on your scanner, but the truth is that you'd probably get just as good results at 1200 dpi or maybe even 800 dpi, depending on the image. There is no magic formula, only experimentation with what works well and what the computer, scanner, and printer can handle. Just remember not to go overboard with a higher resolution than you need; you'll be wasting time.

How to Choose the Proper Resolution

It all boils down to the question, "Which resolution do I pick?" The bottom line is simply to choose a resolution that looks good on the output device.

Table 5-1 lists scanning resolutions for various common types of images. The minimum resolution value is the bare minimum at which you'd want to scan the image and keep it looking good. The "better" value is the "you can get away with this" value, which is a combination of resolution and the amount of time you'll have to devote to image editing. There is no maximum value, since that would be the highest value the scanner can operate at.

Image type	Minimum	Better
Web graphic/JPEG or GIF	100	300
Photo	300	600
Photo (to be enlarged)	600	1200
Line art	300	600
Slides/Negatives	1200	2400
Monochrome images or text	150	300

Table 5-1. *Scanning resolutions (in dpi) for common types of images.*

For example, suppose you want to scan a photo and e-mail it to your relatives. You could get by with scanning it at 100 dpi, but 150 dpi or any value on up to 300 dpi would produce a better image—even for the Internet. (It boils down to the time you want to spend scanning the image.) Anything over 300 dpi would be a waste of information for an Internet image. (If you doubt this, then try scanning the image at 100 dpi and then 300 dpi. It takes less time and looks OK at 100 dpi, but looks much better at 300 dpi.)

Another example: You're scanning an old wedding photograph as a present. You want to enlarge the picture and give it as a gift. From the table, a color photograph (to be enlarged) could be scanned at 600 dpi, but scanning at a higher value (up to 1200 dpi) would be better. In fact, 1200 dpi would give you more than enough detail for editing and touchup, plus enlarging.

The key is never to scan at a higher resolution than you need. Remember: higher resolutions take longer to scan and are clunkier to work with even on the fastest computers. If you can't tell the quality difference in the output, then there's no point in wasting time scanning at those ultimate resolutions.

- "Line art" is a non-photographic image. For example, scanning lil' Jonah's first real drawing of Mommy and Daddy qualifies as line art.

- Scanning black-and-white text or other items can be done at lower resolutions. Because there are no colors in the image, it can be scanned at a lower resolution.

- If you find values other than those listed in Table 5-1 that work better for you, feel free to use them instead. This is all subjective

Digital Scanning and Photography

information, and the output quality on your particular computer and printer should be the best gauge of which resolutions to use.

- If you plan on doing Optical Character Recognition (OCR), then a scanning resolution of 300 dpi is all that's necessary. See Chapter 2 for more information on OCR.

- Incidentally, a fax machine reproduces at 200 dpi. Ugly, huh?

Diving into Color Depth

Walking hand-in-hand with resolution is the oft-misunderstood concept of color depth. That refers to the variety of colors available to the image you scan. Selecting the proper color depth depends on the image you're scanning and the output device, but more than that, color depth plays an interesting companion role to the resolution.

As an example, consider your television. The TV has a very low resolution but nearly an infinite number of colors available. By having more colors available, the TV makes up for its poor resolution. The array of colors smoothes the rough edges at the low resolution, tricking the eye into seeing what appears to be a higher resolution image.

FYI

The monitor's resolution is linked to color depth. Some high resolutions cannot support the 32-bit or 16-bit color depths. This is related to the amount of memory you have on the video card (the more, the better). For photo editing, I recommend 32-bit True Color (or "Millions of colors" on the Macintosh). If that resolution isn't available, I recommend selecting the highest resolution that lets you keep the most colors.

Figure 5-7 was scanned in at 72 dpi. The image on the left was scanned in using only 32 colors—a very low color depth. The image on the right was scanned using 256 colors, which is still low but you can vividly see how only a few more bits of color information make a big difference in how the picture appears. Scanning the image using millions of colors still keeps the low resolution, but with more colors available the detail *appears* finer even at the low resolution.

72 dpi

72 dpi

Low color depth
(32 colors)

Medium color depth
(256 colors)

Figure 5-7. *The effects of color depth on a low-resolution scan.*

How Color Depth Works

Color depth determines how many colors are available in the image. There are several settings, from only two colors (black and white) on up to millions of colors (which I won't list here). The colors are given in two formats, either as a number, such as 256 colors or 16 million colors, or as a depth value, such as 8-bit or 24-bit. Both numbers and depth values describe the same thing, as shown in Table 5-2.

Bit depth	Number of colors
2-bit	2
8-bit	256
16-bit	65,536
24-bit	16,777,216
36-bit	68,719,476,736
42-bit	4,398,046,511,104

Table 5-2. *Bit depth and the number of colors available.*

FYI

Your scanning program may list the color depth by bit values or by the number of colors. The values in Table 5-2 are precise, though your scanning program may specify only "thousands of colors" (16-bit) or "millions of colors" (24-bit or more).

  Digital Scanning and Photography

The color depth values, say either 8-bit or 256 colors, describe the number of colors available for the image. They are not always the same 256 colors, but rather 256 different shades plucked from the entire spectrum. So, for example, if you scanned an image of a tree frog you might have 256 shades of green in your image. Scan a picture of the beach and the 256 colors will probably be a variety. No matter how it sorts out, there can only be 256 colors when you choose a color depth of 8-bit.

Obviously, the higher the color depth value, the better. If you have the option of millions of colors, go for it! The computer can better duplicate and manipulate an image composed of millions of shades than it can a few hundred or thousands of shades. True, it uses more memory, but the results are worth it.

The Special Case of Black-and-White Color Depth

Even though it's called "color" depth, it also applies to any black-and-white images you might scan. A color depth of 2-bits gives you two colors, black and white. This is referred to as a *monochrome* image. A color depth of 8-bits gives you 256 shades of gray. Such an image is a *grayscale* image.

Can you have black-and-white images with a color depth beyond 256 shades of gray? Not really. Even if the scanning program or imaging software will let you create such an image, there is no need for it; 256 shades of gray is enough for any black-and-white image.

Choosing whether to scan in monochrome or grayscale depends on the image source. If you're scanning in an old black-and-white photograph of yours, then grayscale is okay. If what you're scanning is a drawing (commonly called *line art*), then you can get by with monochrome (2-bits, two colors). For example, the instructions for the new anti-gravity device you sketched on a cocktail napkin would best be scanned in a monochrome mode. All you need are black dots for the line art and white dots for the napkin part.

If you confuse things and scan in line art as a grayscale image, you may notice that it looks, well, "dirty." That's usually a sign that you should rescan at a lower color depth, or at 2-bit monochrome.

Most photo editing programs have the ability to convert a color image into grayscale. Doing so simply removes the color information, translating the image into a 256-color grayscale.

Your software might use the term "256 levels" instead of "256 colors" when referring to grayscale.

If 256 shades of gray isn't enough, many scanners offer higher grayscale resolution. A grayscale resolution of 14 bits gives you 16,384 gray levels. Again, that many gray levels may not be necessary or even possible to print.

How to Choose the Proper Color Depth

Choosing a color depth depends on what you're scanning. It's easy to break this into black-and-white and color images.

For black-and-white images you have two choices: grayscale and monochrome. Grayscale can be 256 shades of gray (8-bit depth) or more, depending on the scanner. This is perfect for any black-and-white image, photograph, or original source. Monochrome is only black and white (2-bit depth), which is ideal for line art, plain text, and similar originals.

IMPORTANT

You could scan simple black-and-white images using grayscale color depth. But when you do, the document on disk grows in size. For example, an image scanned at a 2-bit depth may occupy only 32 KB of disk space. A grayscale image may occupy 300 KB or more.

Color images can be scanned at any color level. If you plan on doing a lot of image editing, then the higher the bit depth, the better. Though, as with a high resolution, it does take the scanner longer to work with a humongous bit depth. JPEG and GIF images, however, may need only 216 or 256 colors (8-bit depth).

Task List

1. Review your image's resolution.

Run your image editing program, and open one of the images you scanned from Chapter 4. The method for discovering the image's resolution depends on your image editing software, as shown in Table 5-3.

Application	Method
Imaging for Windows	1. Choose Properties from the Page menu. 2. Click the Resolution tab.
Adobe PhotoDeluxe (Windows)	1. Click the Advanced button. 2. Click the Size tab. 3. Click the Photo Size button.
Adobe PhotoDeluxe (Mac)	1. Click On Your Own. 2. Click the Modify button. 3. Click the Size tab. 4. Click the Photo Size button.
Photoshop/LE	1. Choose Image Size from the Image menu.

Table 5-3. *Commands for finding the resolution of an image.*

In all of the above applications, the image's resolution is shown somewhere in the dialog box. (Be sure to close the dialog box when you're done looking.)

2. Zoom in and out of your image.

First, zoom the image out to 100%. Note how the image's resolution relates to your monitor's resolution (which can be anything from 72 dpi on up to 96 dpi or more). Next, zoom into the image until the dots appear as large blocks on the screen. The higher the resolution, the more dots you'll see. For high resolution images, you may have to zoom in to 800% or more to see the blocks.

3. Compare color depths.

Scan in a color image at an 8-bit color depth. Save that image to disk. Then rescan the same image, but change the color depth to 24-bits or more. (Use the scanning program to do this. You may have to switch to the advanced mode.) Compare the images by zooming in and examining the colors available. If possible, try to compare the images side-by-side. (You cannot compare images side-by-side in PhotoDeluxe.)

4. Compare black-and-white color depths

Sign your name on a piece of paper, and scan it in. First, scan it in as line art, or set the color depth to 2-bit monochrome. Zoom in to see how the image appears in 2-bit mode. Save that file to disk. Next, scan in the image as an 8-bit grayscale. Zoom in this time, and notice how the curves in your signature are more accurately represented by the grayscale.

6

Modifying the Image

Scanning is a lot more complex than using a photocopier, which is a good thing. Not every scan is merely a copy of an original. No, thanks to the power and versatility of your computer, you can *improve* upon the original. This can be done in two places: in the scanning program itself and in your imaging software.

This chapter covers modifying the images you scan. The techniques and examples show you how useful it can be to adjust, touch up, or improve your image before or after it's scanned.

Some Scanning Tricks and Tips

Your scanning program allows you to do more than just scan. Already this book has shown you how to preview, magnify, select, and scan an image. Chapter 5 dealt with selecting resolution and color depth, which is also a function of the scanning program. Beyond that, most scanning programs let you do a few other things to an image before it's transferred to the imaging software for further touch-ups.

Using your scanning program, you can:

- Change an image's size

- Rotate or flip the image

- Change the contrast or brightness or adjust color levels

- Apply a filter

There are probably other tricks you can perform in the scanning program as well. The following sections go into detail on why and how you would accomplish these tricks. Note that not every scanning program is capable of these tricks. (Not to worry; nearly all the imaging or photo-editing programs available can easily handle these tasks.)

Running Your Scanning Program

Before you discover what wonders your scanning program is capable of, you'll need to start that program.

Activate the Scanning Program

1. Run your imaging or photo-editing software.

Popular imaging programs are listed in Chapter 1. Most likely you have either Adobe PhotoDeluxe or Photoshop, though other applications can also work with a scanner.

FYI

You must run the imaging software before you can scan. Imaging software merely opens the door to the scanning program, which is where the actual scanning takes place. Refer to Chapter 4 for a review of how to operate your scanning program.

2. Activate the scanning program.

You should be able to use a command on the File menu to do this, but in some programs you need to click a button on a toolbar. (See Chapter 4.)

3. Switch your scanning program to advanced mode.

If you've been using beginner mode to scan, you should switch to advanced mode now. Clicking an Advanced or More Options button should do the trick.

TIP

If your scanning program lacks an advanced mode, that's fine. It probably has all the options you need, although be sure to check for optional menu items or pop-up buttons that may display more information.

Now you're ready to scan an image and work through the next few sections in this chapter. I'm assuming your scanning program is up on the screen and that you're familiar with its basic operation, as covered earlier in this book.

Changing the Image Size

Your scanning program may be blessed with options for reducing or enlarging the image as it's scanned. Remember that the image is normally rendered at its actual size; scanning a 5-inch-by-5-inch original results in an image that is the same size. However, you can change that size within the scanning program.

For example, suppose you're scanning in a 5-by-3 photograph to post on your Web page. You don't want the image to be that large on the Web page, although half that size would be OK. Within your scanning program, you can set the scale to 50 percent.

Change the Size of an Image

1. Place an image to be scanned in the scanner.

2. Click the Preview button to preview the image.

    The image should appear in the scanning program, ready for action.

3. Reduce the image's size by half (50 percent).

    In the VistaScan program, this is done by selecting 50 percent from the drop-down list, as shown in Figure 6-1. Other scanning programs may have a drop-down list, slider, or text box in which you type the scale for reducing or enlarging the image.

    Note that you may not see the image physically change size. Why? Because you're looking at a preview of the image as it sits in your scanner. You'll see only the smaller (or larger) image after it's scanned and transferred into the imaging software.

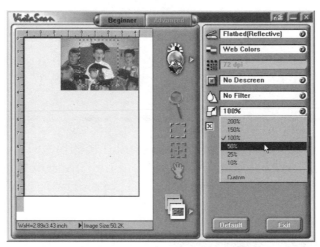

Figure 6-1. *Adjusting the image scale in the VistaScan scanning program.*

Yes, there *is* a relationship between scaling and the image's resolution. The scaling does affect resolution! For example, suppose you're scanning in a 5-by-4 photograph you want to touch up and enlarge. So you're scanning at 600 dpi (a good resolution for editing; see Chapter 5), but you're also scaling the image to 200 percent. That creates a final image with a resolution of 1200 dpi. Yes, this will take longer to scan and edit, and it will create a very large file on your disk. There's nothing wrong with enlarging the image this way, but keep in mind that it does affect the resolution.

At this point you could scan the image at 50 percent of its original size, but since this is a tutorial, you don't have to.

4. Set the image scale back to 100 percent.

You can continue working with the same image in the preview window in the next section.

> **IMPORTANT**
>
> The scanning program will not let you increase the resolution beyond that of your scanner. So, suppose you have a scanner with a maximum resolution of 2400 dpi. In that case, you cannot scan an image at 2400 dpi and scale it to anything over 100 percent. Likewise, you cannot scale a 1200-dpi resolution beyond 200 percent.

Scaling an image as it's scanned is a nifty trick—a real time-saver if you're absolutely sure you need an image enlarged or reduced by a certain percentage. This same trick can be done within the imaging software, though unlike scaling in the scanning program, scaling in the imaging software does not change the image's resolution. That's OK if you want to reduce the image size, but if you plan to enlarge an image, my advice is to do it in the scanning program.

Changing the Orientation

One of the most common things to edit in an image is the orientation. Images often need to be rotated, flipped, or inverted. For example, the only way to fit a large original into the scanner might be to turn it sideways. Using your scanning program, you can rotate that image immediately, so it's fed into the imaging software in the proper orientation.

For this exercise, you can use the image already shown in your scanning program's preview window, or you can place a new image into the scanner and preview it.

In VistaScan, rotating the image is handled using the special multi-use button. The following steps apply to VistaScan only. Your scanning program may have similar controls, a pop-up menu, or a tab to click for rotating the image.

Change the Orientation of an Image

1. Click the multiuse button.

A palette with four different sets of controls is displayed: brightness/contrast, tones, colors, and orientation.

2. Click the orientation tab.

The palette displays nine orientation options, complete with image preview in each as shown in Figure 6-2. Note that some of the images are rotated 90, 180, or 270 degrees, others are flipped left-right or top-bottom, and others are flipped and rotated. There is also an option for inverting the image, that is reversing the colors. This option works best on monochrome images.

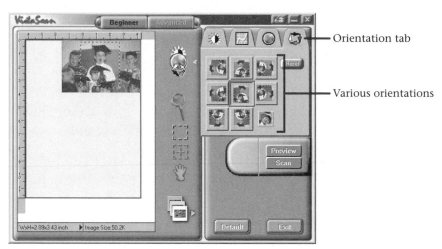

Figure 6-2. *VistaScan's optional palette contains controls for further adjusting the image.*

3. Choose the orientation you desire.

The image in the preview window doesn't change; however, the image appears in the new orientation after it's scanned and has been loaded into the imaging software. You'll confirm this when you finally scan in the image.

  Digital Scanning and Photography

4. Click the multiuse button again to hide the palette.

This is optional, though you'll need to do this in VistaScan if you plan on using any of the options that the palette is currently obscuring.

5. Make any additional changes to the resolution, color depth, size, and other settings as necessary before you scan.

At this point, you're ready to click the Scan button. The image will appear in the imaging software in the orientation you selected. Or, if you like, you can continue working with the same image in the next section.

Rotating the image is usually done in 90-degree increments, clockwise or counterclockwise.

Flipping an image "horizontally" creates a mirror image left to right from the original. Flipping an image "vertically" creates a mirror image from top to bottom.

Yes, rotating and flipping an image can be done in the imaging software as well. The bonus there is that imaging software has an Undo command, whereas if you screw up in the scanning program you'll have to rescan. Also, imaging software usually lets you rotate the image in one-degree increments, which is more precise than the scanning program allows.

Adjusting Brightness and Contrast

Most scanning programs let you adjust an image's brightness and contrast as well as color levels. However, these are things I recommend you do in your imaging software and not in the scanning program. While most scanning programs have this ability, and you can see the results in the preview window, it's just better to scan in an image and mess with brightness, contrast, and color levels in the imaging program where you have more control *and* the Undo command.

If you're curious, you can check out the brightness and contrast options in your scanning program. They're usually labeled with the "contrasty sun" icon, as shown in the margin. In VistaScan, click the multiuse button (the same one used for changing the orientation), and then click the contrasty sun tab to play with or observe the various settings.

Applying Filters and Other Adjustments

One thing done best in the scanning program and not by imaging or photo-editing software is applying filters to an image. Filters let you compensate for some of the shortcomings of your originals.

There are many types of filters—including filters to sharpen the image and blur the image—but first among them is the *descreen* filter (sometimes referred to as an antimoiré filter or interference filter). This filter, which works only in the scanning program and not in your imaging software, is used to remove strange patterns that can appear when you scan some types of images. For example, some original images, such as magazine and newspaper images, are composed of hundreds of tiny dots (a "screen"). Unlike a photograph, which is a continuous tonal image (a fancy term for "no dots"), when you scan in a screened image it produces a *moiré* pattern (say *mwa-RAY*), such as the one shown on the left in Figure 6-3.

FYI

Moiré refers to something that has a rippled surface, like water. Moiré patterns are often used to create optical illusions or interesting visual patterns. In those cases, the moiré patterns are desirable, but when you scan an image they should be removed.

Figure 6-3. *The image on the left has moiré patterns, while the image on the right is improved by using a descreen filter.*

Digital Scanning and Photography

To reduce or remove the moiré pattern, you should select a descreen filter. In Figure 6-3, the image on the right was scanned that way.

The descreen filter in VistaScan is controlled using the Descreen drop-down list, as shown in Figure 6-4. Options are available for common screened image sources, or you can set your own descreen filter using the Custom option. So, for example, if you're scanning a screened image from a newspaper (please review the sidebar "Important Information About Copyrights" in Chapter 4 if you are), you should select the Newspaper, or 85 lpi, descreen filter.

FYI

The abbreviation *lpi* refers to Lines Per Inch, which is related to the way images are reproduced in newspapers, magazines, art books, and other mass-produced materials.

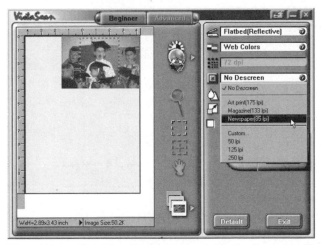

Figure 6-4. *The VistaScan program with the Descreen filter drop-down list displayed.*

Your scanning program may sport other filters as well, though I'm generally of the opinion that any modifications other than descreening should be done in the imaging software instead. For example, VistaScan contains filters for sharpening or blurring the image. Even so, most popular imaging or photo-editing applications contain better tools that let you refine what you sharpen or blur—as well as that highly valued Undo command.

Other Things Worth Noting in the Scanning Program

Each scanning program is subtly different and offers various controls and features to help you scan. For example, one version of the Microtech scanning program has an "image calculator" that helps you estimate the final disk size of the image you scan in (which is irrelevant seeing that the final size really depends on the image format).

Your scanning program might also offer you the option of choosing the image source or scan method for your image. If your scanner has a separate transparency adapter (TA), for example, you may have to choose that source from the scanning program rather than using the glass. Ditto for scanners with automatic document or sheet feeders (ADF). There might also be options to set if you're scanning a color negative. (Note that VistaScan refers to a transparency as a "transmissive" source.)

Finally, if your scanning program is so blessed, you may find an Auto Adjustment option. Selecting this option uses the scanner's own smarts to make all the adjustments necessary for a great scan. You may still have to select resolution and color depth, but many of the other minor details will be automatically selected for you. Nifty, huh?

Photo Editing Tricks and Tips

Your imaging software is designed to help you improve upon the quality and appearance of the images you scan. This is why such software is bundled with scanners and digital cameras. The images you create are OK by themselves, but often you need to do things like save the image in a specific format, print the image, resize, adjust colors, fix problems, add text, or any of a number of interesting things.

The following sections cover many of the popular tricks you can pull with most imaging or photo-editing applications. For more information, you should refer to the on-line documentation or get a good book specific to your software. Try to find books that explain how to do things as opposed to books that merely describe what commands are available.

Getting Started

Set Up Your Imaging Software

1. Scan in a sample image.

   This image can be anything. You just need something you can work with in the following exercises. A color photograph would work best.

2. Set up the scanning program as needed, and then click the Scan or OK button to transfer the image into the imaging software. Refer to the following table for specific instructions on how to set up your program:

Application	Method
PhotoDeluxe (Windows)	1. Click the Advanced button.
PhotoDeluxe (Macintosh)	1. Click On Your Own. 2. Click the Modify button.
Photoshop LE	(There is nothing you need to do here; the program is always in "advanced" mode.)

3. Save the image in the native format.

   The native format provides you with a backup copy on the hard drive should you utterly screw things up.

If you do screw up, close the altered image *without saving*; if your application asks you to save, click No or Don't Save. Then reload the original by using the Open command on the File menu or by using either the Revert or Revert To Saved command on the File menu.

Zooming

One of the most basic functions of any imaging software you should learn right away is zooming. Zooming does not change the actual image's size, it merely makes it larger or smaller on your screen, which helps as you edit.

Most imaging software uses a magnifying glass (not a lollypop) icon as the zoom tool (like the zoom tool in scanning programs discussed in Chapter 4). Choosing that tool changes the mouse pointer into a magnifying glass as well. Just as in scanning programs, the magnifying glass mouse pointer usually has a plus sign (+) in it for zooming in or a minus sign (–) for zooming out. Click the mouse to zoom in, and press the Alt or Option key, and click to zoom out. Additionally, some applications have pop-up or drop-down lists of various zoom percentages: 100 percent is "actual size"; 50 percent is half size; 200 percent is twice as large.

TIP

With some programs, you can drag the magnifying glass mouse pointer over a portion of the image to zoom in to just that portion.

Zoom In on an Image

1. Load an image into your imaging software.

2. Display the image at its actual size (100-percent zoom).
Here are specific instructions, should you need them:

Application

PhotoDeluxe (Windows)	1. Choose 100% from the drop-down list at the top of the image's window.
PhotoDeluxe (Macintosh)	1. Use the zoom-in and zoom-out icons as well as a text box for inputting the zoom value. They are found below the red Help and Undo buttons on the left side of the image.
Photoshop LE	1. On the View menu, click Actual Pixels.

3. Zoom in until you can see the individual dots that make up the image.

The dots aren't "pixels" but rather individual color elements that compose the picture. The amount you need to zoom depends on the image's resolution, though most imaging programs only let you zoom in 1600 percent.

Application

PhotoDeluxe (Windows)	1. Press Ctrl+Plus Sign (+) several times until you see the large color blocks that compose the image.
PhotoDeluxe (Macintosh)	1. Click the "plus sign" button several times until you see the large color blocks.
Photoshop LE	1. Choose the Zoom tool from the toolbox. 2. Click the mouse on the image until you can see the large color blocks.

4. Zoom out until the entire image fits on the screen.

This may be unnecessary if your image already fits on the screen. But some images scanned at higher resolutions will require you to zoom out until they fit on the screen. (You may need to load a higher-resolution image or scan a new image at a higher resolution to best see how this works.)

Application

PhotoDeluxe (Windows)	1. Press Ctrl+Minus Sign (–) several times until the entire image appears on the screen.
PhotoDeluxe (Macintosh)	1. Click the "minus sign" button until the entire image appears in the window.
Photoshop LE	1. On the View menu, click Fit On Screen.

TIP

In Photoshop LE, you can display two views of the same image, which allows you to use the Zoom command to its full ability. On the View menu, click New View. Then use one of the windows to display the image in its actual size, and use the other window to zoom in and edit. That way, you can preview your edits as you make them to see how good they look.

Cropping

Cropping is the fancy art term for trimming an image. You cut away the parts you don't need and are left with a smaller image of what you want—similar to a vengeful teenager snipping her ex-boyfriend from photographs with a pair of scissors.

Cropping is typically done with a cropping tool, such as the one shown in the margin. This tool is dragged over an image to select the part you want to keep. Some programs, however, merely let you select a portion of the image and then choose a Crop command from a menu or use a toolbar to assist with cropping. The following table lists cropping techniques for the three popular photo-editing applications covered in this book.

Application	
PhotoDeluxe (Windows and Macintosh)	1. Click the Size tab.
	2. Click the Trim button
	3. Drag the mouse over the image, selecting the part you want to keep.
	4. Click inside the part you want to keep to crop the image.
Photoshop LE	1. Choose the Rectangular Marquee tool from the toolbox.
	2. Drag the mouse over the image, selecting the part you want to keep.
	3. On the Image menu, click Crop to crop the image.

Note that cropping does change the image's size; the result is a smaller image. But cropping itself is not the same as resizing an image. Here are some cropping tips:

- You can only crop a rectangular area of the image. Though you may be able to select odd shapes, you cannot crop to them. (Refer to the section, "Selecting Parts of the Image" later in this chapter for more information.)

- It might help to zoom into your image as you're cropping. This helps you to crop as neatly as you can.

- Remember that the Undo command can restore your image if you crop badly.

  Digital Scanning and Photography

Rotating

While scanning programs can rotate images before they're scanned, most imaging software gives you greater control over rotating or flipping your images. For example, most imaging software lets you rotate an image in single-degree increments. This often corrects some problems when the image wasn't lined-up perfectly in the scanner.

Application

PhotoDeluxe (Windows)	1. Click the Orientation tab.
	2. Click one of the four buttons to rotate or flip the image. To rotate 180 degrees, click the Rotate Left or Rotate Right button twice.
	3. To rotate by specific degrees, choose Free Rotate on the Orientation menu, and then use the mouse to drag the image clockwise or counterclockwise.
PhotoDeluxe (Macintosh)	1. Click the Orientation tab.
	2. Click one of the four buttons to rotate or flip the image. To rotate 180 degrees, click the Rotate Left or Rotate Right button twice.
	3. To rotate by specific degrees, click the Free Rotate button, and then use the mouse to rotate the image to your liking.
Photoshop LE	1. On the Image menu, point to Rotate Canvas and choose the proper rotation amount or choose the flip command.
	2. To rotate by specific degrees, point to Rotate Canvas on the Image menu, click Arbitrary, and type the amount to rotate the image clockwise or counterclockwise.

Note that rotating the image in increments other than 90 degrees keeps the image in a rectangle. Figure 6-5 shows an image being rotated 45 degrees. See how the background or *canvas* remains the same size; only the image itself is rotated. To eliminate the excess background, either crop the image or enlarge the canvas before rotating to display the entire rotated image. (See the next section on resizing for more information.)

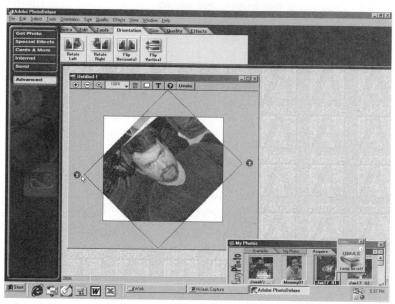

Figure 6-5. *Rotating an image in other than 90-degree increments results in strange cropping.*

Resizing

There are two parts to every image you edit, both of which can be resized. The first part is the image. You set the image size when you scan, either to 100 percent (which makes it the same size as the original) or by adjusting the scale to make the scanned image larger or smaller.

The second part, the canvas mentioned in the previous section, is harder to see. Normally the canvas size and image size are the same. However, you can make the canvas larger or smaller; making it larger gives you room to edit your picture and making it smaller has a similar effect to cropping. More on this in a moment.

First, resizing the image is done in one of two directions: enlarging or reducing. In both cases, you're changing the image's actual size. For example, suppose you scanned in an image you want to post on a Web page. In that case, the image shouldn't be too large or it will take forever to load. Instead, you choose to reduce it to about 150 pixels wide—a good general width for images posted to a Web page. This is not the same as zooming in or out, and it's not the same as cropping.

Digital Scanning and Photography

Resize an Image

1. Load an image into your imaging software if necessary.

2. Reduce the image.

Here are the steps you take in the various imaging applications:

Application

PhotoDeluxe (Windows and Macintosh)	1. Click the Size tab 2. Click the Photo Size button.
Photoshop LE	1. On the Image menu, click Image Size.

Figure 6-6 shows a typical resizing dialog box. Both the image's size on the screen and "actual" size are presented; the top values shown in Figure 6-6 tell how large the image will print, while the bottom values allow you to adjust the size (and even the resolution).

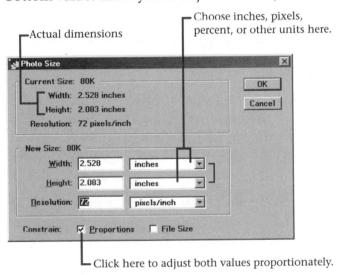

Figure 6-6. *Changing the image's size.*

3. Ensure that the image will be reduced proportionally.

Check to see that a Proportions or Constrain or similar option is selected in the resizing dialog box. You want to ensure that if you change one dimension of the image, the other dimension changes size accordingly.

4. Choose the proper measurement from the drop-down lists. For this exercise, choose pixels from both drop-down lists. (In Adobe Photoshop, choose from the Pixel Dimensions section of the dialog box.)

Imaging software lets you resize the image based on many measurements, all of which are listed in the resize dialog box's drop-down lists. You can resize based on measurements in inches, pixels, centimeters, or other measurements, or you can choose to reduce or enlarge the image by a given percentage.

5. Enter 150 as the new width of the image.

You should see the height value adjust accordingly (provided you've selected the Proportions or Constrain option).

6. Click OK.

The image is resized to a width of 150 pixels. The height has also been adjusted. Note how the image appears just the same, only smaller.

FYI

Reducing an image does not diminish the quality. Enlarging, however, does cut down on the quality—unless you've scanned the image at a higher resolution!

At this point, you could edit the image further, save it to disk as a JPEG or GIF file, or continue editing. But for this exercise you need to undo the change you just made so that you can keep working.

7. On the Edit menu, click Undo.

Now to enlarge the image, repeat the steps above, but this time set the width to 200 percent of the image's current size; choose Percent from the drop-down list, and type 200 as the new size. (Remember, this action makes the image larger; it's not the same as zooming in at 200 percent.)

Note that the image appears larger on the screen—and probably has inferior quality as well. Some images may look good; but unless you've scanned at a high resolution, enlarging the image makes the tiny dots that compose the image larger and easier to see. The moral of this lesson is to scan at a higher resolution if you plan on enlarging the image. So if you're planning on enlarging an image by 200 percent, scan at twice the resolution you would normally use.

8. On the Edit menu, click Undo.

Finally there's the issue of canvas size. Reducing the canvas size results in cropping the image. Enlarging the canvas size creates a blank area around the image. See Figure 6-7 for an example of a Canvas Size dialog box where you can make these changes.

Here are the various steps taken to adjust the canvas size:

Application

PhotoDeluxe (Windows and Macintosh)	1. Click the Size tab. 2. Click the Canvas Size button.
Photoshop LE	1. On the Image menu, click Canvas Size.

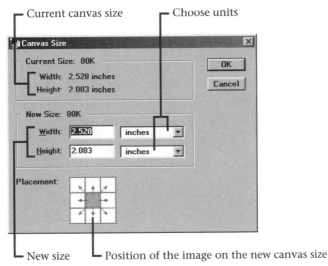

Current canvas size   Choose units

New size   Position of the image on the new canvas size

Figure 6-7. *Changing the canvas size is done in this dialog box.*

As with changing the image size, you can choose a specific set of new measurements for the canvas height or width, or you can reduce or enlarge by percentages.

Change the Canvas Size

1. Choose Percent from both drop-down lists, and then type 150 into both text boxes to set the canvas size to 150 percent.

Note that there's no Proportions or Constrain setting here; changing the canvas size does not change the size of the image. This step makes the new canvas one-and-a-half times as large.

When you choose to reduce the canvas size, a warning dialog box may appear. It alerts you that the image will be cropped by the smaller canvas size.

2. Click OK.

   The image should be surrounded by a large blank border. That's the new canvas. Now, for example, you could rotate the image 45 degrees and not crop it.

3. On the Edit menu, click Undo.

   The canvas returns to its original size.

You may refer to enlarging an image as "blowing it up." This is improper terminology. To sound professional, use "enlarging" instead of "blowing up." Demolition people blow things up.

One instance in which you may need to reduce the canvas size is when printing an image for a specific size. For example, if you have a special frame that's exactly 4 inches by 5 inches, you can adjust the canvas size to 4 inches by 5 inches, print the image, and see how it fits in the frame. This is much more precise than cropping.

Adding Text

A popular trick to pull for sending images via e-mail is to add text. If you're good, you can even create cartoon bubbles and put the text in them. But for now, here are the tools for adding text to an image:

Application

PhotoDeluxe (Windows)	1. Click the Text Tool button (the capital "T") on the image's window.
PhotoDeluxe (Macintosh)	1. Click the Tools tab.
	2. Select the T, Text button.
Photoshop LE	1. Choose the Type tool from the toolbox.
	2. Click in the image where you want the text to appear.

Creating Wallpaper

Wallpaper is the background image you see when you use Microsoft Windows. Yes, you can use your scanner and imaging software to create custom wallpaper for your computer. It's actually quite easy.

1. Find out the dimensions of your desktop. In Windows, open Control Panel, double-click the Display icon, and click the Settings tab to obtain the desktop's dimensions. On most computers, it's probably either 800-by-600 or 1024-by-768 pixels. That's the size you need for the desktop image. (You could make the image smaller and "stretch" it, but you'll get the best quality if the image is exactly that resolution.)

2. Scan an image for the wallpaper. The resolution you choose depends on the image's size. If the image is the same size as your computer's monitor, scanning at 100 dpi would be fine. If it's half as big, 200 dpi is OK; if it's one quarter the size, scan at 400 dpi, and so on. You want to have enough information available should you need to enlarge the image.

3. Resize the image. Set the image size to the same size (in pixels) as the computer's display. This can be tricky because the image probably doesn't have the same horizontal-to-vertical proportions. If this is the case, make the image slightly larger. For example, if you set the new image size to 800 pixels wide, the height value may be 659 pixels—too high for the desktop. But that's OK. As long as the image is larger than the desktop size, you can crop.

4. Resize the canvas (if necessary). If the image is larger than the screen size, resize the canvas to exactly the same number of pixels as the desktop. This will crop the image to exactly fit on the screen.

5. Save the file as a Windows Bitmap or BMP graphics file. Save it in the Windows folder on your hard drive, giving it a proper name.

6. Return to Control Panel, double-click the Display icon, and click the Background tab to choose your new wallpaper from the list.

A dialog box should appear, similar to the one shown in Figure 6-8, which allows you to type and format the text. This may seem weird to you if you're used to other graphics programs that let you type directly on the image; in photo-editing applications, the text is usually formatted in a dialog box before it's placed on the image.

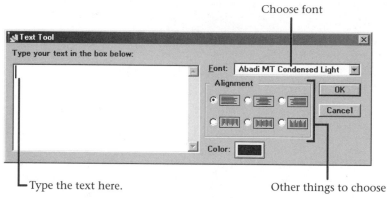

Figure 6-8. *A dialog box for creating and formatting text for your image.*

Add Text to an Image

1. Type the text.

   The text you type should be appropriate to the image, though I've found that the text "Burp!" can be applied to just about any image you have.

2. Format the text using whatever options suit your fancy.

   Pay special attention to the color. For example, black text may not show up on your image, so white or gray may be a better alternative.

3. Click OK.

   What happens next depends on which program you're using. PhotoDeluxe puts the text in a floating box, as shown in Figure 6-9. You can drag the text around in the image, stretch it, or rotate it. You can even double-click the text to edit it.

   In Photoshop, the text is put on a new "Layer" in the image. It can be moved or edited separately from the rest of the image (which lies beneath the text). (Refer to the Photoshop help or to a good Photoshop book for more information on dealing with text or layers.)

   Now you can save the image, print it, or whatever. Or just close the image's window to do another tutorial.

  Digital Scanning and Photography

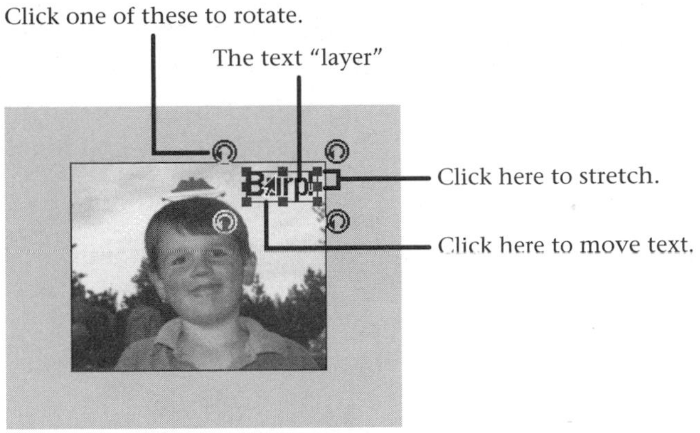

Click one of these to rotate.

The text "layer"

Click here to stretch.

Click here to move text.

Figure 6-9. *Adding text to an image in Adobe PhotoDeluxe.*

Adjusting Brightness and Contrast

Before going into the how-tos of brightness and contrast, a brief orientation is necessary.

Adjusting brightness changes the amount of light and dark areas in the image. It will not "add more light" to a dark original, but it can be used to lighten the highlights or darken low-lights. Figure 6-10 illustrates various settings for brightness.

Figure 6-10. *The center image has no brightness adjustment, images on the left have their brightness decreased, and images on the right have brightness increased.*

Making the Cartoon Bubble

If you want to put the text into a cartoon bubble, you must first draw the bubble using one of the image-editing program's drawing tools. If an Oval or Line tool is available, you can use that. Otherwise, you'll have to use the Brush tool and white "paint" to create the oval.

After the cartoon bubble is drawn, slap down the text. (Of course, there are more steps involved, but I don't have the space here to explain them all. Just don't forget your Undo command!)

Adjusting contrast changes the difference between the light and dark areas of an image. Too much contrast, as shown in Figure 6-11, results in a choppy, almost two-tone image. Too little contrast washes the entire image out, resulting in a rather flat, gray appearance (also shown in Figure 6-11).

Figure 6-11. *No contrast adjustment was made to the center image; images on the left were flattened with less contrast, and images to the right had their contrast increased.*

TIP

Usually it's a balance of both brightness and contrast adjustments that create the best image.

Change the Brightness and Contrast of an Image

1. Load an image to test the brightness and contrast settings, or you can use any image you're currently playing with.

You can open a file already on disk or scan in a new image. If possible, try to scan a grayscale image, which best illustrates brightness and contrast settings.

2. Summon the brightness and contrast settings dialog box.

Adjusting brightness and contrast is usually done in the same dialog box. Here are the instructions for getting there:

Application

PhotoDeluxe (Windows and Macintosh)	1. Click the Quality tab. 2. Click the Brightness/Contrast button.
Photoshop LE	1. On the Image menu, point to Adjust, and click Brightness/Contrast.

3. Ensure that the Preview option is on.

You want to see the changes as you make them, which is accomplished in most imaging software by clicking on the Preview option.

4. Adjust the brightness values up and down.

5. View the changes in the image as you drag the brightness slider with the mouse. Be sure to check the settings, both brighter and darker. (You have to release the mouse button to see the changes.) Note how positive values indicate a brighter image and negative values are for a darker image.

6. Type **0** into the text box to reset the brightness value.

7. Adjust the contrast value up and down.

See how the positive values result in a more contrasty image while negative values give you a flatter image.

8. Type **0** into the text box to reset the contrast value.

9. Click OK to close the dialog box.

Brightness and contrast effects can also be applied in the scanning program, but scanning programs lack an Undo command.

Many image-editing programs also have the ability to let you adjust brightness and contrast for specific parts of an image. Refer to the program's documentation or a good book for details.

FYI

Most imaging software also includes tools for adjusting the color balance, hue, saturation, color curves, channels, and other miscellaneous image aspects. Basically all this stuff can be used to improve the image, but the gory details are best left to books specific to image editing.

Selecting Parts of the Image

Most image editing takes place on only a small portion of the image. Let's say you have a family portrait you need to lighten up Grandpa, who always sits in the back and tends to fade into the background. In that case, you can select only Grandpa's portion of the image and apply a little brightness or contrast to bring him out.

The best tool for selecting a portion of the image is the Lasso or Polygon tool. That lets you select an irregular part of the image for specific editing.

Select Part of an Image

1. Open or scan a new image, or you can continue to play with any image already in your imaging application.

2. Choose the Lasso or Polygon tool. This is done differently in each program:

Application	
PhotoDeluxe (Windows)	1. On the Select menu, point to Selection Tools, and click Polygon
PhotoDeluxe (Macintosh)	1. Choose Polygon Tool from the pop-up list, located under the Select tab on the left side of the window.
	2. Click the New button under the pop-up list.
Photoshop LE	1. Choose the Lasso tool from the toolbar (or press the L key).

3. Select a small part of the image.

    Find a tiny, irregular-shaped part of the image, such as someone's head or an object in the image. Use the mouse to carefully drag the selection tool around that part of the image. To make selecting easier you can hold down the Ctrl key (or Option key on the Mac), and then click the selection tool at various points around the image to control exactly which parts you select. You may find this easier than dragging the mouse.

4. Double-click the mouse when you're done selecting.

This closes the selection, creating a separate region in your image for editing. Now all the painting, filters, and other commands you use in the image apply only to the area you selected.

Deselect the area using the following steps.

Application

PhotoDeluxe (Windows)	1. Type Ctrl+D.
PhotoDeluxe (Macintosh)	1. Click the None button under the Select tab on the left side of the window.
Photoshop LE	1. Type Ctrl+D (Windows) or Command+D (Mac)

Remember, any effects you apply to the image take place only in the selected area. So once Grandpa is selected, you can lighten him up and no one will ever accuse him of lurking in the background.

Copying and Cloning

You can copy, cut, and paste parts of your image just as you copy, cut, and paste text in a word processor. The difference is that cutting graphics does not "squish together" the rest of the image. No, it leaves a hole in the image. The moral: If you're going to cut and paste people's heads in a photo, make sure all their heads are the same size.

One unique way to copy graphic information is to use the clone tool or image stamp. That tool takes one part of the image and copies it to another part. For example, in Figure 6-12 you see the before and after effects of cloning.

Original image

Cloned fire truck

Figure 6-12. *The fire truck from the original image (left) is cloned to create a duplicate in the second image (right).*

The clone tool can also be used to fix old photographs. You can copy and paste to fix cracks, tears and scratches. You can also fix discoloration by selecting parts of the image and applying brightness/contrast, or by painting. (Don't be disappointed if your efforts here don't match your expectations; digitally retouching photographs is something professionals get paid lots of money to do.)

Copy or Clone an Image

1. Start by selecting the clone tool.

Here's how that's done:

Application

PhotoDeluxe (Windows)	1. Click the Tools tab. 2. Click the Clone button.
PhotoDeluxe (Macintosh)	1. Choose the Rubber Stamp tool from the toolbar, or press the S key.
Photoshop LE	1. This tool is not available in the current version of Adobe Photoshop for the Macintosh.

In PhotoDeluxe (Windows), a target appears in the image. That's the source target, showing from where the information will be cloned.

2. Choose the source.

This is the location of the original material, the stuff you're copying.

Application

PhotoDeluxe (Windows)	1. Use the mouse to drag the source target in the image.
Photoshop LE (Windows)	1. Press the Alt or Option key, and click the Rubber Stamp tool in the image

3. Paint with the clone tool.

Drag the mouse where you want the image copy. If you're unsure about this, just move the mouse away from the source and start dragging it around. You'll see how the original is repainted at the location where you're dragging the mouse. You can adjust how much of the image is cloned by choosing a different brush shape from your application's brush palette. This is how cloning works.

You can also choose a second source by resetting the source target and then painting again. I had to do this in Figure 6-13. That's my little brother and me in the original image (Figure 6-12). By resetting the clone tool to several places, I was able to erase my little brother from the tub. Don't I look happier?

4. Close the image.

Save it to disk if you like, otherwise you're done with this tutorial.

Figure 6-13. *Cloning can even put an end to any sibling rivalry.*

Touching-Up or Painting

There's just something funny about blacking out someone's front tooth in a photograph. Of course, Mom may have gotten mad—but that was probably because you defaced a photograph. When you do the same thing to a scanned photograph, you're just defacing pixels. So blacking

Digital Scanning and Photography

out a front tooth or drawing a moustache is not only possible, it's considered acceptable.

Paint on an Image

1. Load in image, preferably an image of a person.

2. Choose the paint brush tool.
   Here's how to find it:

Application	
PhotoDeluxe (Windows and Macintosh)	1. Choose the Tools tab. 2. Click the Brush button.
Photoshop LE	1. Choose the Paintbrush tool from the toolbar, or press the B key.

   You're not ready to draw yet. Next you need to select the color you're painting with.

3. Select a brush size using a brush-size palette similar to the one used in the previous exercise. (You may need to reset the size after you start painting.)

4. Select a color using the following steps.

Application	
PhotoDeluxe (Windows and Macintosh)	1. Click the Color button in the Brushes palette. 2. Click to choose a color from the Color Picker window.
Photoshop LE	1. Click the foreground color part of the Foreground Color/ Background Color button (near the bottom of the toolbar). 2. Click to choose a color.

If you want to choose a color that's already in the image, you need the eyedropper tool. Here's how to select it:

Application

PhotoDeluxe (Windows and Macintosh)	1. Click the Color button in the Brushes palette. 2. When the Color Picker window is displayed, point the eyedropper mouse pointer into the image. 3. Click the spot in the picture that contains the color you want to use
Photoshop LE	1. Choose the Eyedropper tool from the toolbox, or press the I key 2. Click the spot in the picture that contains the color you want to use.

5. Drag the mouse over the image to draw. As you drag, the paint brush tool draws in the size and color you selected.

IMPORTANT

You cannot draw on a Photoshop image that has been saved with a 42-bit color depth. To change the image back to RGB format, on the Image menu, point to Mode, and click RGB Color, and, if necessary, point to Mode, and click 8 Bits/Channel.

Other Things To Do

Are you having fun yet?

Playing with images is a great way to, well, waste time. Sure, it's "research." And, alas, since this book can only be so big I don't have the space to cover all the nifty tricks you can do with your imaging software—not to mention other add-ons provided by Kai's Power Goo and similar fun applications.

You can play on your own with just about any part of the imaging program. As long as you initially save the image or use the Undo command, you can't screw anything up. So have fun with the filters or drawing tools. Enjoy yourself!

Don't let your imaging software frustrate you. These programs are complex and learning them takes time. I've been using Photoshop for ten years now, and I still know only 20 percent of the program.

For more information on how to do what in your imaging program, refer to a good book on the subject. Try to avoid books that merely document what each feature does. Instead, pick up a book that tells you how to do various tricks.

Task List

1. Scan in an image for enlarging.

   Whatever the original's size, scan and print a duplicate twice as large. Remember you need to double the resolution in the scanning program and enlarge the image in the imaging software.

2. Add text to an image.

   Find an image with two people and scan it in. Add text to the image so it looks like they're talking to each other.

3. Use the clone tool to modify an image.

   After you play with the clone tool for a while, set out to really do something with it. Take an image of a park and duplicate one of the trees, or an image of a skyline and duplicate one of the buildings. Or use the cloning tool to fix scratches or blemishes on an older photograph.

7

Selecting a Digital Camera

Stuff covered here

Understanding digital film
Choosing a proper digital camera
Discovering the megapixel
Storing images in the camera
Transferring images to the computer
Noting other important features

Scanners may be popular, but the biggest buzz in the digital imaging forest comes from the busy hive of digital photography. Of all the wondrous gadgets in the world, the digital camera is truly the most wondrousful. And it has everything a gadget geek loves: It does something useful, does it quick, interfaces nicely with the computer, and most importantly it looks very, very cool.

On the nuts-and-bolts level, a digital camera is really nothing more than a handheld portable scanner. Most of the technology is, in fact, identical. The other differences—pro and con—plus general buying advice can all be found nestled in this enthralling chapter.

All About Digital Film

If you can work a typical 35mm SLR camera (SLR is just fancy talk for "I paid more than $200 for this thing"), you can probably handle any digital camera on the market. Some digital cameras have more gizmos and controls than others, but anyone can learn how to use all those dials and knobs, or you can just ignore them, which is what I do. But before learning the details, you should familiarize yourself with the concept of *digital film*.

Digital cameras, of course, don't use any film. So digital film is nothing more than images stored electronically, just as they're stored inside your computer. The result of this is that there's no developing in a digital camera. It's all instant. This is even better than a Polaroid camera. No wait-and-peel! What a perfect gizmo for the impatient consumer of today!

The following sections mull the pros and cons of digital film, which should help you decide whether or not you're ready to take the digital plunge.

- Aside from the digital film difference, these cameras resemble their film-based cousins and generally operate in the same manner. Some of the models even use the same lenses, filters, and other attachments that their film counterparts do. Most can cut off Aunt Edna's head just like film cameras have been doing for over 100 years.

- SLR means single lens reflex, which means the camera shows you the same image the camera sees.

What Do You Mean by "Digital Camera"?

The information in this chapter specifically pertains to digital *still* cameras. Though many of these cameras are also capable of capturing video images (which are really several still images in sequence), this chapter does not cover digital video cameras specifically.

Some digital video cameras may be capable of taking still images, and some of the information here may apply to them. But digital video is an entirely different arena with problems, issues, and solutions all its own.

The Rewards of Digital Film

When film made its debut more than 100 years ago, it was explosive. Literally. The chemicals used to create film could, under the right conditions, blow up. (And I don't mean "enlarge.") Then along came Kodak with its "safety film," which had the ability not to blow up. Not much else has changed in the film arena since the dawn of the digital film age just a few years back.

FYI

Kodak's negatives once had "Safety Film" right on them. Betcha always wondered why.

Just as safety film had advantages over the exploding film of an earlier age, digital film has many advantages over its chemical-based counterpart. Here are several of the more popular reasons for going digital:

- **Digital film is eternal.**   As long as there are good batteries in the camera, or the image has been transferred into a computer, the original pictures are intact and can be used over and over again. Traditional film can fade, scratch, get stepped on, melt and, of course, explode if it's old enough. (By the way, they haven't made exploding film since the early days of photography, so those old negatives grandma has should be perfectly safe.)

- **Making copies of the pictures is easy.**   To make a copy of a standard film print you need the negative, the negative's number, plus a developer. With digital film, you just print another copy of the image stored on your computer.

- **You can "delete" images you don't like.**   Most digital cameras have a Play or Preview feature. This lets you see the image you just took or review all the images stored in the camera. If you don't like an image, you can erase it right there in the camera, making room for more images.

- **Cheaper than buying film.**   After the initial purchase, using a digital camera doesn't incur any further costs. True, new batteries may cost something, but not as much as purchasing film every time you want to shoot. And you'll never be out of film as long as you remove pictures you don't want or transfer pictures to your computer. Even the cost of extra memory is cheaper in the long haul than constantly buying and developing new rolls of film.

- **It's fast.**   There is no developing time for digital film. You see the results instantly.

- **It won't explode.**   'Nuff said.

The Perils of Digital Film

Most digital film disadvantages have to do with the underlying technology, which is flat-out expensive. For the cost of a typical digital camera, NASA could send a cat into space. Seriously, like any technology, the prices should come down in time and the technology you can get for

  Digital Scanning and Photography

those prices should be pretty good. Until then, here are a few digital film disadvantages:

- **Chemical-based film holds the best image.** Just as some audiophiles prefer old LP records (analog) over newer CDs (digital), there are true advantages of traditional film (analog) over the digital variety (digital, of course). First, film always has a higher resolution. While it's hard to tell with smaller photographs (especially 4-by-6-inch prints with a photo printer on high quality paper), if you plan on enlarging the images over 8 by 10 inches, digital film looks, well, digital. Second, film can do some tricks digital can't, such as low-light exposures, long exposures (say, of a lightning storm), and double exposures. You can fake some of these tricks by using photo-editing software, but "real" film still does a better job.

FYI

Keep in mind that chemical film is also widely available and cheap. If you're on safari there's probably a hut nearby that sells Kodak or Fuji film, but trying to find a computer to upload your digital camera's images will be tough.

- **The cameras are expensive and tend to be complex.** No doubt about it, the latest and best digital camera is going to cost you much more than its traditional film counterpart, maybe more than your house payment. And they are complex! Digital cameras seem to be loaded with buttons and knobs, often labeled with international symbols, strange icons or the annoying multifunction button that makes setting the time on a VCR seem simple. Add to that the insult of advancing technology; you pay a lot today for a camera that will be utterly obsolete in a few years. I bought my first digital camera for $800, and it wouldn't fetch $50 today—even with those pictures of Elvis still in it.

- **Images must be transferred and stored in the computer, which takes time and uses disk space.** This is the extra step that makes using a digital camera more of a pain; you must set aside time to move the images into the computer for further manipulation. They're making it easier than in the old days, but it's still a required step that occupies your time. (Thought for the future: Maybe someone will invent a combination digital camera/cellular phone for instant uploads to the Internet? Hmmm . . .)

- **You must print the images.** Some traditional film developers accept digital cameras (or their film storage devices) and do all the printing for you, sometimes at high resolutions and on very fancy printers. That can be nice. Some special photo printers can accept digital camera input and print the pictures directly. Otherwise, it's up to you to do the printing. Again, that takes time.

- **Batteries are more important.** It's not that losing the battery will kill off all the images in the camera; for most digital cameras, that isn't true. But digital cameras use a lot more battery power than film cameras, so dealing with batteries becomes more of an issue.

The bottom line is that digital photography is still evolving. The cameras are expensive because the technology is new. Yet even newer technology will leapfrog the current stable of digital cameras, rendering them obsolete in just a few years. Most people would rather sit this game out than waste a bunch of money on what is essentially an expensive toy. Ain't nothin' wrong with that.

How to Choose a Digital Camera

Buying a film camera can be cheap and easy. A $20 camera can get the job done, and disposable 35mm cameras have captured too many vacation pictures to mention. But if you want *really* nice images, you have to pay more. And what you're paying for are all the knobs, gizmos, and photographic lingo that comes with taking those very nice pictures.

Selecting a nice film camera can be daunting, but it's rather tame when compared with choosing a digital camera. In addition to all the basic photographic jargon, you add on a whole host of new electronic and digital terms.

Here's the short list of things you'll need to know about as you fish in the digital camera sea. Each of these is covered later in this chapter:

- What's a *megapixel*?

- How are the images stored in the camera?

- How do the images get into the computer?

- What other features are worth noting?

- Anything else you need to know?

Funny, but "how much will it cost" isn't a necessary question on the list. That's because there's only one real price for a digital camera: *expensive*. You get a lot for that price, and you shouldn't expect to find any bargains or deals on a nice digital camera. Maybe the prices will be competitive with traditional cameras in a few years, but they are not now.

Most decent digital cameras sell for $600 and up, with the average being about $800. You might be able to get some older models for $500 or less.

If you're just interested in a digital camera for taking pictures for the Web or to send via e-mail, you might be able to find a bargain unit for under $300. But taking low-resolution Web page images is about all the camera is good for.

By the way, it makes no difference whether you have a Macintosh or PC when you buy a digital camera. All cameras work with all computer platforms.

The Megapixel Question

It's come to pass that digital cameras sold today have one feature touted above all others. That is the *megapixel*. To understand this, you need to understand the basic concept of image resolution (so a review of Chapter 5 may be in order).

First of all, know that film cameras don't have an issue with resolution. A typical 35mm camera uses film that is 35mm wide (1 3/8 inches). The image itself appears in a rectangular part of the film, the part that's exposed to light when the camera's shutter snaps open and closed, as shown in Figure 7-1.

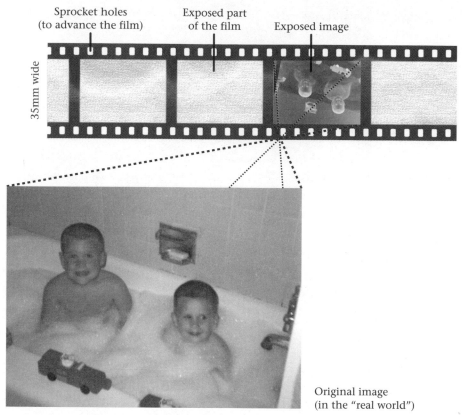

Sprocket holes
(to advance the film)

Exposed part
of the film

Exposed image

35mm wide

Original image
(in the "real world")

Figure 7-1. *A typical strip of 35mm film; the film's chemicals capture the image as exposed by the camera's shutter and focused by the camera's lens.*

When a digital camera snaps a picture, the resolution you select determines the size of the image. Low-resolution images are smaller and require less memory, so the lower the resolution of your images, the more images the camera can store. If you snap images at the highest resolution, the camera can store only a few images.

Table 7-1 shows the short list of common digital camera resolutions.

Resolution	Good for
320 x 200	Not much. This resolution works well only for tiny images.
640 x 480	Web page images and GIFs or JPEGs you plan on attaching to e-mail messages.
1024 x 768	High-quality 5-by-7-inch prints.
1280 x 1024	Images you want to enlarge to 8-by-10-inch prints.

Table 7-1. *Typical digital camera resolutions.*

Digital Scanning and Photography

So what's a megapixel? It's defined as a grid containing one million pixels. Technically that's an image with a resolution of 1024 by 1024 pixels. (That's equivalent to scanning a 5-by-7-inch picture at a resolution of about 200 dpi.)

Today is the era of the multi-megapixel, with 3-megapixel cameras considered the current "high end." These cameras can capture an image on a grid composed of 3 million pixels, which is about 1732 by 1732 pixels. (An 8-by-10-inch photograph would have to be scanned at a resolution of approximately 200 dpi to achieve a 1732-by-1732-pixel resolution.) In many cases, the multi-megapixel cameras rival their film counterparts in quality images.

Choosing the proper resolution for your needs depends on the output device. If you're just snapping a few pictures for an Internet photo album, saving money and buying a lower resolution digital camera is a wise choice. But if you plan on "joining the twenty-first century" and dispensing with your old film-based cameras altogether, you'll need to pay a little more to get the same quality.

IMPORTANT

Beware of "interpolated" resolutions. This is where software is used to enhance lower optical resolution. For example, a digital camera may have only a 1024 x 768 resolution, but through various tricks it might be able to approximate or "guess" a higher resolution and therefore boast some obnoxious megapixel value. Base your purchase decisions on the camera's true optical resolution—instead of that interpolated resolution—when shopping.

Some digital cameras require you to store all the images at one resolution; others let you mix and match resolutions. Make a note of this if mixing and matching resolutions is a feature you like.

As with scanners, the resolution you select in your digital camera depends on the output device. So if you're snapping photos for the Web, you can set the camera to a lower resolution to be able to take (and store) more pictures. But if you are using the digital camera for wedding photography, you're better off settling for fewer images at a higher resolution.

How the Image Is Stored Inside the Camera

Digital film isn't wound up on a spool. No, it comes in one of two flavors: electronic memory storage, similar to the RAM in your computer, or disk storage, similar to the disk storage in your computer.

Memory Card Storage

The typical digital camera uses some type of electronic memory on which it stores the images. This memory comes in the form of a *memory card*, which is a wafer-thin dealie that slides into the camera body. The memory card is capable of storing anywhere from 4 MB on up to 320 MB of information.

There are two types of memory card widely used: CompactFlash (CF) and SmartMedia (SM). Figure 7-2 illustrates a typical CompactFlash card.

Figure 7-2. *A typical CompactFlash type of memory card.*

Each type of memory card has various descriptions and pros and cons and la-di-da. Your camera will use either SmartMedia or CompactFlash. The only time you should care which is which is when you need to buy a new memory card. Make sure you don't buy the wrong kind, as the two card types are incompatible.

Once you know which type of memory card your digital camera uses, adding more memory (photo storage) is as easy as buying a second memory card or a memory card with a higher capacity. The memory cards aren't really that expensive, either. So go ahead and buy a second or third card for your camera. Expect to pay only a few dollars per megabyte.

- If your computer has a memory card adapter, you can plug the memory card into the computer to instantly access the images.

- Memory cards do not require batteries. They will retain their images forever—or at least until nuclear war breaks out.

- Some digital cameras may use memory storage but not have a removable memory card. This wouldn't be as good as a camera with removable storage.

FYI

The number of images the camera is capable of storing depends on the amount of memory or storage inside the camera as well as the resolution of the images you take.

Disk Storage

The second form of digital camera storage is disk storage. Even this varies a bit—from cameras that use standard 3 1/2-inch floppy disks to cameras with teensy tiny specialized drives.

The advantage to having a camera that uses 3 1/2-inch floppy disks is that it's easy to transfer the images to your desktop computer, which also sports a standard 3 1/2-inch floppy drive. (Floppy drives are optional add-ons for all iMacs and G4 Macintoshes.) Also, 3 1/2-inch disks are cheap! You can stock up on them at any office supply store so that you'll always have enough "film."

On the downside, 3 1/2-inch floppies don't hold much information. So you might be able to fit only four (or fewer) high-resolution images on each disk. Also, floppy disks are extremely unreliable and make for bad long-term storage, which is why Zip drives and SuperDisks are being used as alternatives on many computers. If you use floppy disks, however, I suggest transferring the images to your computer's hard drive as soon as possible, lest you lose anything. (Floppy disks typically wear out after about six months of constant use.)

Other than floppy disks, some digital cameras also employ tiny, removable hard drives, which fit right into the camera. There are also specialized storage devices, such as Iomega Clik! and other disks that can be read by both the digital camera and your computer.

From the Camera to Your Computer

This is what drives everyone nuts: getting the images from the camera into the computer. This isn't a problem if you think about it *before* you buy the camera, since you can actually ruminate on which camera-to-computer method would work best for you. But too many people are stuck with a "bargain" digital camera only to find out that connecting it to the computer is akin to assembling a backyard swing set with a hammer and duct tape.

Here are the six ways to get the pictures out of a digital camera, ranked in order from least effective to most effective:

- **Use the TV.** Many digital cameras have a "TV-out" connector, which you can use to plug directly into a TV or VCR. You can then play the images in the camera on the TV and record the images on videotape as well. But you're not going to get them into the computer that way. Personally, I know of no one who's done this.

- **Use a serial port.** Most computers have one or two serial ports, which can be used to transfer images in from the camera. If you already have a modem or some other device connected to the serial port, that means you have to switch cables. Since the serial port is on the back of most computers, this becomes a pain. It's also the slowest way to get the images into the computer. (And keep in mind that newer Macintoshes and some new PCs lack serial ports.)

- **Use a USB cable.** USB (universal serial bus) cable is the latest, greatest way to get your computer to talk to a variety of devices. Connecting the computer to a camera with a USB cable is a snap, literally! The images flow into the computer via a special camera-reading program, and then you can do with them what you will. Then you can disconnect the camera (without turning the computer off) and venture out into the world for more pictures.

- **Use FireWire.** The FireWire connection works just like the USB connection, athough it's much, much faster. The downside is that few cameras and even fewer computers are equipped with a

FireWire port. This should change in the future, but it remains the fastest way to transfer images into the computer today.

- **Use a photo printer.** If you just plan on printing the images, you can squirt them directly into a photo printer, providing you have such a printer and that your camera has the ability to format and send the images that way. This doesn't save the images on the computer's hard drive, which is the only drawback. (You still need to send the pictures to the computer if you plan on saving them long-term.)

- **Use the same media the image is stored on.** The very best way to get your images into the computer is to have the computer read the camera's storage device directly. For example, you remove the memory card, 3 1/2-inch floppy, or other disk storage device from the camera, and then plug it into your computer. Ta-da! You have instant access.

If you plan on doing a lot of digital photography, I recommend getting a device for your computer that can read the memory cards *and* getting a photo printer for instant hard copies.

The USB cable connection works best if your computer has a USB port. Check this out before you buy a USB-cable camera.

Most digital cameras come with several different types of cables plus the various output connectors to use them. Not only is this handy to have, but it allows you to use the camera with different computers that might have different connectors.

Other Worthy Digital Camera Features

The list of features for a digital camera is far longer than the features for a typical SLR camera. For example, I have a nice film camera I bought a long time ago and, though I use the thing all the time, I haven't a clue as to what half the buttons and knobs do. This problem is compounded on a digital camera, which has extra knobs and buttons for resolution and other electronic settings. It's enough to make you nuts.

Before going nuts, here's the short list of other digital camera features worthy of a look:

The Image Sensor Type

The digital camera is nothing more than a handheld scanner, and as such it uses the Charge-Couple Device (CCD) or Contact Image Sensor (CIS)/ CMOS technology to capture the image. As a rule of thumb, a camera with a CCD type of image sensor will be better than a camera with the CIS or CMOS type. (Refer to Chapter 2 for more information on the image sensor.)

Battery Issues

Like most cameras, a digital model requires batteries to keep it up and running. Unlike regular cameras, however, digital cameras gulp up battery juice in a thirsty hurry. (The liquid crystal display [LCD] is the main culprit here.) Because of this, you may find your digital camera running through batteries at a fast clip.

While cameras that use standard AA batteries may seem like a deal (since the batteries are available everywhere), my advice is to find a camera that comes with rechargeable batteries. This works best if the batteries can be charged while they're in the camera; just plug the camera into the wall when you're not using it and it should always be ready.

TIP

Try to avoid NiCad (Nickel-Cadmium) rechargeable batteries. NiCads retain a battery "memory" and tend to lose their recharging abilities over time. Instead, look for NiHM, Lithium-Ion, or "air" batteries, which don't have the memory problems of NiCads. Also try to get a camera that uses standard-sized batteries, rather than specific photo batteries. Standard batteries are easier to find and replace.

LCD Panel vs. Optical Viewfinder Cameras

Picture-taking has come a long way since the days of the old Brownie Box cameras where images in the viewfinders appeared upside down and backwards. Today, the better cameras are of the SLR type, which means the image you see in the viewfinder will be exactly the same image that's exposed on film. Other, non-SLR cameras use a see-through type of viewfinder, which only approximates the image.

Figure 7-3 illustrates the differences between a viewfinder and an LCD. The viewfinder shows you only a close approximation of the final image. With an LCD, the camera lets you accurately frame and preview the final image.

Viewfinder approximation

Actual image

LCD shows the actual image.

Figure 7-3. *The viewfinder lets you see the image without showing you how it's framed. Only with an LCD type of camera can you see exactly what you'll get.*

The advantages of using a viewfinder on a digital camera are that it's cheap and doesn't hog battery power. In bright light situations, an LCD can get "washed out," which leaves you little choice but to use the viewfinder (if the camera has one). Also, the viewfinder lets you hold the camera like a traditional camera, which some people find easier than the camera-at-arms-length-I-look-like-I'm-over-40-and-need-reading-glasses approach of the LCD.

In addition to being able to preview and frame the image, an LCD has the advantage of letting you preview or "play" the images recorded in the camera. Obviously, the larger the LCD is, the better it can be used this way. But as the LCD increases in size, so does the cost of the camera.

- An LCD is a sort of mini-flat-screen monitor for your digital camera.

- I recommend getting a camera with both an LCD and viewfinder. Remember that framing and cropping can always be done later in your photo-editing application.

- Some cameras have special LCD options that let you view the image even in bright light.

- Some digital cameras have a flip-around viewfinder or lens that lets you easily take a picture of yourself. This is much better than trying to use a desktop scanner on your face.

Hello, Camera! Can You Hear Me?

For some reason, many digital cameras come with a built-in microphone. That way you can make digital audio recordings or comments on the pictures you take.

"Darlene, you closed your eyes again! I swear you did!"

"Don't photograph my belly!"

"Oscar, just *try* to smile, OK?"

"Cheeeeeezzzz . . ."

Yes, I'll grant that this is an odd feature to have. I believe the microphone is really a what-else-can-we-toss-in type of gadget on a digital camera, more of a marketing decision than something you'll truly use. But if you're interested in adding sound to your images, pick one of those cameras. (The audio is recorded separately from the image, and is transferred to the computer using the software that comes with the camera.)

Lens Options

If you pay a sack of gold for your camera, you might find that it works with standard photographic lenses, such as those made by Nikon or Canon. If you're like most of the digital camera crowd, however, you'll most likely be stuck with whatever lens comes with the thing. If so, try to get a camera with a wide-to-telephoto zoom lens.

The wide part of the lens is what lets you see a lot of information up close. For example, if you're standing close to the thing you're taking a picture of, the wide setting would be best. Wide lenses work best for close-up objects, indoor pictures, and close-ups.

The zoom part is what lets you see images far away. Is your neighbor sunbathing again? Use the zoom lens and find out.

Zoom lenses are gauged by their *zoom power*. For example, a 3X zoom lens can enlarge or zoom in to an image three times the size it appears when viewed with the naked eye.

Some zoom lenses have *macro* ability. That means you can zoom in to objects that are very small and photograph them so they appear larger. For example, you could use the macro lens to zoom in to a bee on a flower and capture and enlarge the bee's expression as it gets angry and turns on you.

Avoid cameras that offer a "digital" zoom lens as opposed to an optical zoom lens. A digital zoom lens basically uses the camera's software to crop a normal image, making it appear close-up. This is not a true zoom, as the image loses resolution when the camera enlarges it.

Other Photographic Features

Just about anything that applies to a standard camera also applies to a digital camera: shutter speed, lens aperture, depth-of-field adjustments, self-timers, built-in flash, red-eye reducer, and so on.

Pay special attention to the camera's focus. Some digital cameras are *fixed focus*, which means the focus is preset and cannot be changed (like any disposable vacation camera). Some cameras may have a manual focus, but most people prefer and I recommend an automatic focus. Yup, you'll pay more for that.

Oh, and I'm sure the salesperson will be glad to list all the various features of all the cameras they have in stock. From this point on, you've crossed from the digital hills into the valley of basic photographic mumbo jumbo. You can listen intently to the salesperson at this point, but all the information you need to know about purchasing a digital camera is explained in this chapter.

And, of course, don't forget the handsome, leatherette carrying strap.

A Few Final Thoughts

Until this area of computing evolves or the technology settles down, I can't really offer any more details or suggestions. As with buying anything, always check the service and support policies. Each of these are common questions you should ask when you buy anything high-tech:

- Where can the camera be fixed? Right there at the store is best, though most cameras will probably have to be shipped to a repair facility.

- Who do you call for help? This should be either your local dealer or camera store, or an 800 number.

- Can it be returned? If it can't be returned, you should be allowed an exchange or credit. Places that don't have such policies should be avoided.

If you're happy with a certain brand name of film camera, you might consider buying the same brand of digital camera. Or if your computer, printer, or hard-drive manufacturer offers a digital camera and you trust their name, you might buy that brand.

Also consider what bundled software comes with the camera. For example, if you already have Adobe Photoshop, you might consider a camera configuration that comes with some other imaging software or maybe some extra add-on such as Kai's PhotoSoap or Super Goo. Or in the same vein, try to find something that's compatible with the software you already have. That should save some learning time.

Task List

1. Review your needs for a digital camera.

   Be honest: Do you really need one? If you can get by with your traditional camera and a good desktop scanner, you're probably set—especially if you're a photographer by nature, why switch? A digital camera is an expensive toy, so you should plan on using it quite a bit if you eventually do fork over the cash.

2. Peruse the various advertisements to see what's available.

   Digital camera technology is leaping forward rapidly, so what's new and what's yesterday's refurbished junk is hard to tell. Remember that the computer industry likes to hype new technology that either might not be available yet or is simply too expensive to be practical. Still, magazine and Internet ads may lead you to some bargains.

3. Buy a digital camera.

   If you decide to step into the digital photography age, buy yourself a camera. For review, consider the following when you do:

   - How many megapixels does the camera sport (or what is its highest resolution)?

   - How are the images stored inside the camera?

   - What methods are used to get the pictures into the computer?

   - Does the camera use a viewfinder, LCD, or both?

   - What other photographic features will you need?

   The idea is to be so well informed that you make the proper decision and buy the best digital camera for your needs.

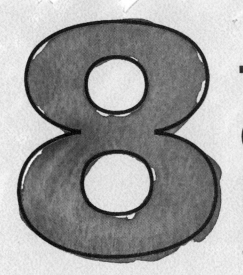

8 The Field Guide to Digital Photography

Stuff covered here

Setting up your digital camera

Preparing for the picture

Reviewing and deleting images

Moving pictures into the computer

The computer is the tool without true parents. It has its roots in electronic calculators and typewriters, but resembles the typewriter in looks only (and even then barely). The reason for this is that the computer wasn't designed to go out and solve any one problem. It does many things and does them well, but there's no specific poison for which the computer is an antidote. Thankfully this isn't true with digital cameras.

A digital camera is designed to be a direct replacement for whatever camera you're working with today. Sure, it's expensive. So what! The point of the thing is to take pictures and store them electronically instead of on film, and just about every digital camera available does that job with amazing ease. If you can use a point-and-shoot camera, using a digital camera is just as easy—with the exception of a few minor issues, which are carefully described in this chapter.

Setting Up the Camera

Pretty much every film camera sold today is of the 35mm type, which means that any little film kiosk in any little grocery is bound to have lots of little canisters full of little rolls of film for any Joe's camera. We can thank aggressive marketing from the Kodak Corporation for that.

With digital cameras, everything is different. There is no standard camera and therefore no standard setup. You'll have to follow the instructions that came with the camera to do the following:

- Charge and install the batteries

- Insert the memory card or internal disk drive (if any)

- Attach the lens (if needed)

- Attach the lovely leatherette carrying strap

Everything should come with the camera, with the possible exception of batteries. If your camera takes standard AA type of batteries, you should consider buying rechargeable batteries as described in Chapter 7.

TIP

If you have a rechargeable battery, follow the battery-charging instructions carefully! Some cameras can plug into the wall and charge their batteries that way; others may have a separate charging unit. Heeding the charging instructions in the manual is important, because you don't want to do anything to the batteries that will shorten their useful life.

Carefully install the memory card or internal disk storage, whichever your camera uses. If your camera uses 3 1/2-inch disks, prepare them as required by the camera (for example, format them if necessary).

Finally, become familiar with your camera. You should locate the following items on the camera body:

- The lens

- The viewfinder (if available)

- The LCD panel (if available)

- The place where the batteries go

- The place where the electronic storage device goes

- The various connectors for getting the image out of the camera, plus a connector for adding a power cord

- The digital information display (if available)

- The screw hole in the bottom of the camera where you can easily attach the camera to a tripod

FYI

The digital information display is a common feature on any advanced camera. It generally tells you how many exposures are left and whether the flash is activated, and it provides you with exposure statistics, battery status, and other information. This data is often displayed using symbols; you'll need to know what the symbols represent. For example, on my EPSON PhotoPC camera, resolution is indicated by a series of stars: One star is the lowest resolution (640 by 480 pixels) and 3 1/2 stars is the maximum resolution (1984 by 1488 pixels).

Finally, familiarize yourself with the buttons and controls on your camera. It may take a bit of effort to figure them out; camera companies often label them using symbols not normally found in nature. Figure out the buttons now, before you go picture-taking, lest you miss some great shots. Here's a sampling of the buttons you should be familiar with:

- The shutter button, which actually snaps the image

- A button that puts the camera into "record" mode, making it ready to take pictures

- A button that puts the camera into "play" mode, which allows you to review the images stored in the camera

- The power button, which might also be the button to set record or play mode

- A button that sets the image quality

- A button that activates or controls the flash

- A self-timer button

- A zoom or wide-angle control button

- Buttons that allow you to manipulate a menu or information on the LCD

- Other buttons for setting the date and time and adjusting other aspects of the camera

There! Now you're ready to go out and shoot something.

Flashing in Public (and Private)

Using the flash on any camera is something of an art form. The following basic flash rules apply to both digital and traditional cameras.

Use the flash at night and in dark situations to illuminate your subject. Remember that film (even digital film) is light sensitive. So even though your eyeballs may see the image, you'll probably need a flash for proper exposure.

Use the flash in daylight or bright situations when your subject is in the shade or against a very light object. This is known as *fill-in flash*, where the flash works to illuminate the subject well, even though the sun is shining.

Using a flash in a stadium or in any situation when you're more than 20 feet away from the subject is a waste of battery power. The flash works well only for things up close and will have little affect on objects 20 or more feet away.

Most cameras have a "red-eye reducer," which shines or blinks a light rapidly before taking the picture. This eliminates the red eye you often get with flash photography (though any photo-editing software can do the same thing). Personally I don't use the red-eye reducer since it adds a time lag between the time I press the button and the time the picture is taken.

You should also have the ability to disable your camera's flash should you ever need to. If you *want* an image to come out dark or you're in a situation where a flash would be inappropriate, such as any of those places where they say, "Flash photography is prohibited," it's probably OK to snap the picture without the flash.

Taking a Picture

For decades, the camera industry has prided itself on "point and shoot." This is ironic because the earliest cameras were all point and shoot. Over time, cameras donned lenses that could focus and apertures that could change size. Shutters could operate at different speeds for better exposure. Photographers wanted more control, but consumers wanted something simple and easy to use. I mean, if your goal in taking a picture is just to paste an image of half of Uncle Thad's face into a photo album, you're not going to care about an f-stop or depth of field.

Your digital camera should be very easy to operate on a basic photographic level. Most digital cameras are auto-focus and auto-exposure, so you can, in a fashion, just point and shoot. Still, you should be aware of some resolution issues plus a few other tips, each of which is covered in the following sections.

Choosing the Resolution

Before you shoot, determine the image's resolution. Remember, the resolution you choose affects the number of pictures you can store in the camera. Figure 8-1 illustrates this using the digital readout on my EPSON camera.

Low resolution
640 x 480

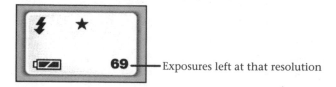

Exposures left at that resolution

Medium resolution
1600 x 1200 (medium compression)

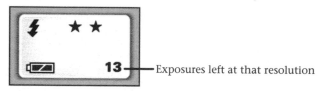

Exposures left at that resolution

High resolution
1600 x 1200 (low compression)

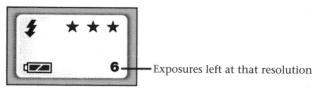

Exposures left at that resolution

Figure 8-1. *The higher the resolution, the fewer images the camera can store. At lower resolutions, the camera can store more pictures.*

Again, the image resolution you select depends on the resolution of the output device, be it the screen or printer. For example, if you're snapping photos for the Internet, the lowest resolution your camera offers will be fine—and you'll be able to store lots of images. For images you plan on enlarging to 8 by 10 inches, a higher resolution is required.

You can always delete images in the camera to give yourself more room for additional photos.

Some cameras may not let you mix and match resolutions; you must set a single resolution for all the images you snap. In that case, settling on a higher resolution would be best since you can always reduce the image's resolution (or size) in the photo-editing application.

Digital Scanning and Photography

Framing the Image

Your next step is to frame the image. With most cameras, you use a viewfinder or LCD or a combination of both to do this.

Using a viewfinder will be comfortable for you if you're used to traditional cameras. If so, try to overframe the image—in other words, ensure that there's plenty of room around your subject so you don't cut anything off.

Using an LCD allows you to perfectly frame the image; what you see in the LCD will be exactly what's captured electronically inside the camera. Framing is a cinch, but holding the camera becomes a bit awkward. You must hold the camera at arm's length to see the LCD. Making minor framing adjustments in that position is tough.

I prefer to alternate between viewfinder and LCD. For sports or action shots, using the viewfinder works well. You can crop the image properly in the imaging program. But for posed photographs, using the LCD guarantees that I'll get everyone in the picture.

Click!

Taking the picture is done in the traditional way: click the shutter button. Some cameras may even play an audible *click* noise to entertain you. (Digital cameras use an electronic shutter and not a mechanical one, so the noise is simulated.)

Note that most digital cameras require time to digest the image you've just snapped. The time required depends on the resolution you've selected; higher resolution images may take up to two seconds to record. This means you must sit and wait for two seconds before you can take another picture. (I know, it's not a long time, but when you have to wait it may *seem* like a long time.)

Once your camera is ready, you can continue taking images just like a regular camera, using the zoom lens, flash, and other adjustments the camera may offer. Some cameras let you take brief videos, others may let you shoot several frames in a row, and still others may let you record audio, as discussed in Chapter 7. Whatever. Have fun.

Note that you can take pictures as long as the camera is in the record mode. To view the images you've taken on the camera's LCD, you need to switch to play mode, which is covered in the next section.

Playing Back the Images

In play mode, your camera lets you review the images you've just taken. This is a wonderful feature, formerly available only to Polaroid camera users. Some professional photographers actually take Polaroid shots of their subjects before exposing traditional film to confirm that the framing and lighting work. Digital cameras allow you to do the same thing—without having to purchase and tote around two separate cameras.

A button or switch on your camera should activate play mode, which displays the images on the LCD. You can use various buttons on the camera to review each of the images stored there, as illustrated in Figure 8-2. (Keep in mind that this is a generic illustration, and your camera probably works differently.)

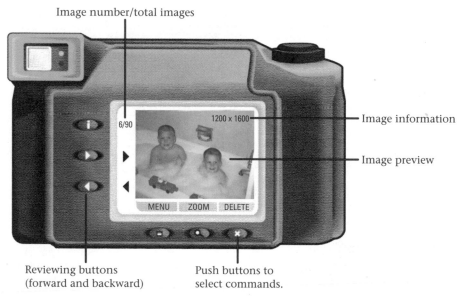

Figure 8-2. *The LCD screen is your main method for reviewing and even editing the images stored in the camera.*

A button or menu option might also be available to allow you to preview multiple images on the LCD, like sort of a mini–photo album. You might also be able to zoom in to the image and scroll it around to confirm details, such as whether Jordan has closed his eyes *yet again*.

After you're done previewing photos, don't forget to switch the camera back to record mode if you plan on taking more pictures. One of the most common foibles of digital camera photographers is forgetting to switch back to record mode. That's most likely because film cameras lack such a nifty feature.

  Digital Scanning and Photography

Deleting Images

If the picture is ugly, embarrassing, or just not what you want, you can zap it! This carefully removes the image from the camera's memory and frees up that memory for taking more images. This is probably the nicest feature of a digital camera. If you can suffer the pain of deleting your own images, you'll ensure that everything left in the camera is exactly what you want.

Deleting an image is done in play mode, when the camera displays its images on the LCD. One of the buttons or menu items available is Delete. Choose that option or press the proper button to remove the picture. The camera may ask you to confirm the image deletion, either by means of a Yes or No menu item or by pressing a special button. Do so and the image is gone!

IMPORTANT

Unlike deleting a file from your computer, you cannot un-erase an image deleted from your digital camera's memory. If you're unsure, don't delete the image!

In practice, you'll be deleting a lot of images from your camera. Any images you take will stay on your camera even after you send them to the computer, so at some point you will need to delete the images in order to take new ones. Hopefully it won't be accidental.

Getting the Pictures into the Computer

Ah-ha! The long-held secret. Yes, there is a way to get the images out of the camera and into your computer. The method depends on the camera, of course, and how the images are stored.

Transferring 3 1/2-inch Floppies

If you have one of the cameras that uses 3 1/2-inch floppy disks for storage, moving the images is simple.

1. Remove the disk from the camera.
   Follow whatever instructions came with the camera for spewing out the disk.

2. Insert the disk into your computer's floppy disk drive.

3. View the contents of the disk.

- In Windows, double-click the My Computer icon on the desktop, and then double-click the icon for your floppy disk drive.

- On a Macintosh, the floppy disk's icon appears right on the desktop. Double-click it to open the icon and display its contents.

4. Move the files onto the hard drive.

Select and drag the image icons from the floppy disk to a proper folder on your hard drive. In Figure 8-3, you see images being dragged from the floppy disk drive over to the My Pictures folder on the hard drive.

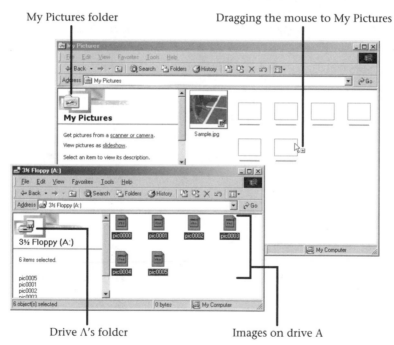

Figure 8-3. *Dragging images from the floppy disk to the hard drive is an important and necessary step toward saving your images long-term.*

Some cameras may require you to run special software that extracts the pictures from the floppy disk. If so, you'll need to run that program to read the floppy disk and transfer the images to a folder on the hard drive.

Digital Scanning and Photography

5. Remove the floppy disk.

When you're done with the floppy disk, remove it from the computer's floppy drive. You should then prepare or reformat the disk to take more pictures.

Using a Memory Card Reader (or Similar Device)

If your camera uses memory cards or some other type of removable storage, you should look into getting some type of "reader" device for your desktop computer. This is the easiest way to get images from the camera and onto your computer's hard drive.

The specifics differ for each type of storage device, but essentially you remove the memory card or disk from the camera and plug it into the computer. From there, either you run a special program to read the device or the device simply appears on the desktop or My Computer window and is accessed like any other storage device in your computer. Transferring the images is then as quick and simple as moving files between two disk drives.

Connecting the Camera to the Computer

Unfortunately, most digital cameras require users to tie their cameras to their computers using some form of electronic umbilical cord. The images stored in the camera are then "beamed" into the computer, which requires some setup but doesn't take that much time.

The techniques for transferring the pictures differ from camera to camera. The first step is always to install the camera's software onto the computer:

1. Install the camera's software.

The camera should come with some basic image-transfer program, one that either works by itself or is *TWAIN-compatible*, which means it works in conjunction with a photo-editing program such as Adobe Photoshop.

TIP

You don't have to install all the software that comes with the camera. For example, I installed only the EPSON Photo!3 program that came with my camera. The other applications that came with the camera? I don't need them.

2. Plug your cable into both the camera and the computer to connect them.

3. For this step, use whichever cables work between the computer and your camera. If your camera has a USB cable, connect the cable to the USB port on your computer. If the camera uses a FireWire, serial, or proprietary cable, connect it instead. Be careful to note whether the computer must be turned off before you can connect the cable!

4. Turn the camera on.

   The camera should be set to play mode or it may have a special "send" mode for talking with the computer. If you have a USB or FireWire camera, the computer will detect it and install it automatically, using the software you've already installed on the hard drive.

Now you're ready to beam!

Installing a Digital Camera with Microsoft Windows Millennium Edition (Me)

The latest, greatest version of the Windows operating system, Windows Me, has a friendly home for digital imaging plus a useful wizard to set everything up. It all starts in the Control Panel:

1. On the Start menu, point to Settings, and click Control Panel.

   This displays the Control Panel, in which you should find the special Scanners And Cameras folder, as shown in Figure 8-4. If you don't see that folder, you can make it appear by clicking the text that reads View All Control Panel Options.

Add Device

2. Double-click the Scanners And Cameras folder to open it.

   You should find the Add Device Wizard sitting in this window, plus any other scanners or digital cameras already installed on your system.

If your digital camera already shows up in the window, great! You're all set. If you don't see an icon representing your camera, you'll need to run the Add Device Wizard to set everything up; double-click the Add Device icon to start the wizard, and follow the instructions on the screen.

Digital Scanning and Photography

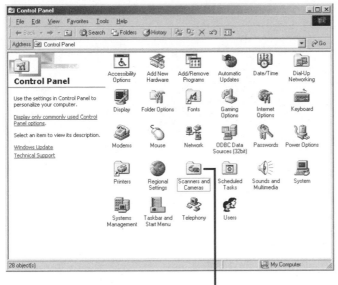

Scanners And Cameras folder

Figure 8-4. *The Control Panel in Windows Me contains a special folder just for your digital imaging needs.*

Transferring the Photos

After connecting the camera, you're ready to transfer the images into the computer. This is accomplished using a special application specific to your camera. For example, my EPSON camera uses a program called EPSON Photo!3 to read the images from the camera and eventually save them to the hard drive.

Another technique is to run your photo-editing program and have it access the software that reads images from the camera, similar to the way the scanning program is run to use a scanner. For example, in Adobe Photoshop (Macintosh) you can choose Acquire and then Twain from the File menu to access the images in the camera. Other applications may have a Get Photo button or Camera menu that lets you access the images.

Figure 8-5 shows the EPSON Photo!3 program reading images from my digital camera. Most camera-reading programs have a similar interface, listing the images in the camera in a preview format. The next step is to select images for downloading and find a proper place for them on the hard drive. (The process is similar for all cameras, but the actual commands might differ.)

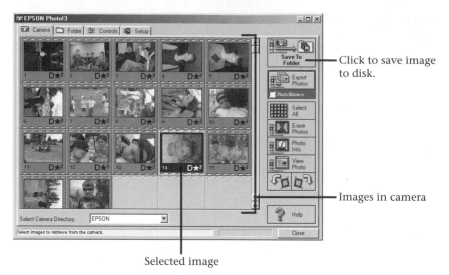

Click to save image to disk.

Images in camera

Selected image

Figure 8-5. *This program reads images from the camera and displays them for transfer into a photo-editing program.*

Here is an outline of the steps you'll take to grab the images:

1. Connect the camera to the computer.

2. Turn the camera on.

3. Set the camera to "send" mode (if available, or play mode or whatever the camera requires).

4. Run the software to read images from the camera.

5. Select an image or group of images to save.

6. Save the images to the hard drive.

7. Optionally delete images from the camera.

Quit the software when you're done, and don't forget to turn off the camera! If you unknowingly leave the camera on, you'll drain the batteries. That's a bad thing.

After the images have been saved to the hard drive, you can touch them up, print them, e-mail them, or whatever. The camera's memory or storage device can then be emptied, allowing you to venture out and snap more digital images.

TIP

Image editing with digital photos works just like image editing with a scanner. Refer to Chapter 6 for all the details.

Digital Scanning and Photography

Task List

1. Go out and take some pictures!

Experiment with using the viewfinder and the LCD, and try different resolutions to see how they affect image storage in the camera.

2. Delete an image inside the camera.

On purpose, take a really awful shot of someone. Show them the preview on the LCD, which should up their dander some. Then show them how quickly and elegantly you can delete the image right there inside the camera.

3. Transfer the images from your camera into your computer, saving them on the hard drive.

The steps for this procedure are unique to each camera, so follow along as best you can with this chapter, making notes of the program names and commands that are specific to your situation.

9 Images and the Internet

Stuff covered here

How to size an image for the Internet

Whether to use GIF or JPEG

How to e-mail an image

You might not have noticed, but the price of scanners dropped just as the Internet became a tremendously popular thing. Coincidence? Probably not. Even though digital cameras make for better Web pictures, they're expensive, so most folks will probably retain their traditional film cameras and use scanners to post images on the Web. Not only that, you can scan in *old* photographs and post them for the world to see. Now everyone can see that you used to run around the yard naked at age three. Oh, parents . . .

I've decided to dedicate this final chapter of the book to images and the Internet, which is probably where most of your digital imaging efforts will end up. This is simple stuff—if you know what you're doing. If you don't know, well then, that's why I wrote this chapter!

Formatting Images for the Internet

You beamed with pride as you scanned in your first image. You decided to proudly announce your new abilities by sending that image off through cyberspace to a friend. After doing that, you probably discovered three annoying things:

- The image file was huge and took forever to send.

- Your friend could not open the image file, after eagerly awaiting its 17-minute download.

- No one considers you a "computer genius" anymore.

Uh-oh. What went wrong?

Yes, you scanned the image properly. Yes, you saved it to disk. And, yes, you managed to send it through the Internet. None of these is a minor feat. But the problem came when you saved the image to a disk. You probably saved the image in the program's native format or the TIFF format. These formats are great for storing detailed information, but they're humongous disk hogs. That's not good for the Internet.

The Internet has to send vast amounts of information through what are essentially tiny pipes. A TIFF file is about the size of an elephant, and squeezing that file through the Internet's tiny pipes is almost like squeezing an elephant through a garden hose. Yes, the elephant will arrive intact on the other end of the hose, but it will take a huge amount of time and effort to move him there.

FYI

The size of the Internet's "pipes" is technically referred to as *bandwidth*. *Wide bandwidth* means you can send lots of information quickly. *Narrow bandwidth* means the information travels slower. Alas, at this stage of the game, the Internet is mostly carried via narrow bandwidth. Somewhere scientists in white lab coats are working on this bandwidth problem.

To deal with the narrow bandwidth problem, the Internet's designers devised some interesting schemes. Most of the Internet consists of plain text files. Just about any Web page you view is nothing more than a text file, with special formatting codes called *HTML* (Hypertext Markup Language) that make that plain text file look interesting when viewed through a Web browser. Plain text takes very little time to transfer over the Internet.

In addition, images on the Web are all of the GIF or JPEG type. These two image formats store lots of information in a compact file size, which helps such images travel through the Internet's narrow bandwidth in an expedient manner. So a JPEG image is like a pill bug, rolling easily through the Internet's garden hose–sized pipes and arriving at the other end quickly and with little effort.

There's nothing wrong with sending huge files through the Internet. It's done all the time. But there's no point in doing so if there's a better, faster solution. Sending a TIFF file when a JPEG would do is wasting time and bandwidth. (This is why many programs you download are compressed into Zip or StuffIt files; those files are smaller than the originals and can travel quickly and smoothly through the Internet's pipes.)

Sizing the Image

The first thing you should do with an Internet image is size it properly. A big mistake made by most first-timers is leaving the image in its original size as scanned. This results in a large image that takes a long time to view—totally unnecessary when you plan ahead.

1. Scan in an image for the Internet.

You can also use a digital camera to capture an image. Whatever the origin, the image eventually ends up in your imaging software.

2. Use the imaging software to resize the image.

What's a good size? It depends on the image, of course. Most monitors have a horizontal resolution somewhere between 640 and 1600 pixels across. An average size for most images, therefore, is about 300 pixels across. Some images may look better at a larger or smaller size, but 300 is a good place to start.

If you want the image to appear larger, choose a larger size. For example, when sending out the family portrait, you might find that a horizontal size of 600 pixels looks best because it allows you to see everyone in the image. That's great! If you want the image to appear smaller, set the number of horizontal pixels to something less than 300, and set it to 200 pixels wide for a vertically oriented (tall) image.

Check the image size on your screen by setting the imaging program's Zoom to 100 percent. Or if there is an "actual size" command, use it to examine how the image looks.

3. Save the image to a disk.

Finally, you need to save the image to disk. This is key! The image must be saved in the GIF or JPEG format, which is covered in the next section.

These are general guidelines for sizing Internet pictures. There's nothing wrong with making the image a larger size, but folks will appreciate the smaller sizes when your Web page loads quickly and they can see the image right away.

The typical computer monitor is set to a resolution of 800 by 600 pixels. Any image larger than 800 pixels horizontally *or* 600 pixels vertically is definitely too big.

Of course, you can send an image of any size to someone via e-mail. If you're working with graphics and someone *needs* a TIFF or Adobe Photoshop–formatted document, you can save the image in that format and send them the file. But if you're just e-mailing friends some pix of the kids, GIF or JPEG is best.

Choosing GIF or JPEG

There is a difference between the GIF and JPEG image formats. It's a subtle difference that's not easy to explain, but it's easy to show.

GIF is perhaps the most versatile of the two Internet graphics formats. It can render full-color or grayscale images, plus line art, drawings, and illustrations, by using a small file size and, darn, the pictures look great. This makes it sound like the only format you need, but GIF does have some limitations.

Perhaps the biggest limitation of the GIF format is that it uses only 256 colors for each image, while JPEG images use millions of colors. This means the GIF image appears "flat" when compared with a similar JPEG image side by side. Some parts of the GIF image may also be dithered. Figure 9-1 illustrates how this looks when the image is zoomed in on, which shows the dithering effect more dramatically.

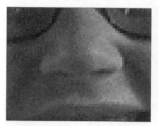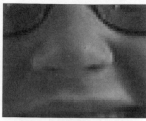

Figure 9-1. *The GIF image (left) uses dithering to make up for its limited palette of 256 colors. The JPEG image (right) has many more colors—and looks better—despite both images being scanned at the same resolution.*

GIF images shine with illustrations, line art, or other types of created images (as opposed to photos, or "real life" images). In Figure 9-2, I scanned in my signature and saved it as both GIF and JPEG images. You'll notice that the GIF version is cleaner and more realistic, whereas the JPEG image has "fuzz" around it.

Figure 9-2. *The GIF image (left) more accurately renders the line art than the JPEG image (right).*

The JPEG image in Figure 9-2 looks crummy because JPEG isn't designed to represent artwork. JPEG is designed to render continuous-tone images, like photographs. It does this by compressing the image—mathematically fitting more information into a smaller size—so that the files don't take up acres of hard drive space.

The compression JPEG uses is referred to as *lossy*. In other words, by compressing the image, the JPEG format does not accurately retain the exact original. Fortunately, due to the nature of the image (a continuous-tone photograph, hopefully), the loss of information isn't that noticeable. So when you save an image in the JPEG format, your software compresses the image into a compact file. And, yes, some of the information is lost. But when you open the JPEG image, it's decompressed and the result is a good-looking image that doesn't consume a lot of disk space.

  Digital Scanning and Photography

The only downside to the JPEG scheme, as seen in Figure 9-2, is that artwork and nonrealistic images are improperly displayed. The compression of my signature caused some information to be lost. Such compression wouldn't affect a photograph, at least not to the point where it would annoy you.

Bottom line: Most of the time you should use the JPEG format for your images. If, however, you're sending scanned artwork or you notice some of your images appear fuzzy, you should consider using the GIF format for that image instead.

JPEGs and Compression

As I said earlier, JPEG images are compressed, which lets them retain a lot of colorful information and not pork up on disk space. There are ten levels of compression quality you can use when you save a JPEG image, from low (1) to maximum (10). When saving a JPEG image, a secondary dialog box appears after the initial Save As dialog box that lets you choose the compression quality.

Low quality (3 or less) gives you a very small file on disk, but the file lacks a lot of the detail found in the higher levels of quality. The image looks OK from a distance, but if you zoom in you'll notice large graphics chunks and "fuzz." At the maximum quality setting (9 and 10), you get very nice, colorful images that look good when enlarged—but the file takes up more disk space.

A good compromise for saving Internet files is to choose a quality setting of 6 or "high." This ensures the JPEG image will have lots of color and detail, but it still keeps the files within a reasonable size.

Sending Images via E-Mail

After the image is properly sized and saved in either GIF or JPEG format, you're ready to send it off into the ether. This is done by attaching the saved file to an e-mail message. So you need several things:

- Internet access, an e-mail account, and e-mail software

- The image file, already saved to disk as a GIF or JPEG

- The e-mail address of the person you're sending to

- A message to send them

The first item is obvious: Without access to the Internet, an e-mail account and an e-mail program, you're not going to send anyone an e-mail attachment. Duh.

Hopefully, you've already scanned the image you want to send. You've also read through this chapter and have properly sized the image and saved it to disk as a GIF or JPEG.

The rest of the things you need are the same as if you were sending any old e-mail message, with the addition of attaching a file to that message. You can attach images to e-mail in all e-mail programs (even AOL and Yahoo!), but I only have room to cover one program so I'll use Microsoft Outlook Express, which comes with all Microsoft Windows and most Macintosh computers. (If you have another e-mail program, it should work similarly to the basic steps outlined below.)

1. Press Ctrl+N (or Command+N on the Macintosh) to create a new e-mail message in Outlook Express.

The New Message window appears, eagerly awaiting your input.

Type the e-mail address of the person to whom you're sending the message in the To field.

You can also click the To button and use the address book in Outlook Express to find a recipient.

2. Press the Tab key until you reach the Subject field, and type a proper subject.

This could be as mushy as, "Here is yet another picture of our adorable child," or you could be subtle and say, "Picture." If you want to be technical, say "JPEG image at quality 7."

3. Type the message text in the body of the message.

You don't have to say much. You could describe the image, just say "hello," or write a regular message.

The tricky part is to actually add the image. This isn't so tough, providing the image has already been saved to a disk.

4. Click the Attach File button.

The Insert Attachment dialog box appears, as shown in Figure 9-3. Use this dialog box to locate the image file you want to send.

The My Pictures folder is a good place to look.

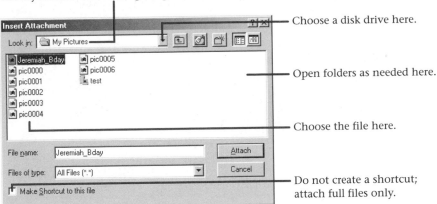

Choose a disk drive here.

Open folders as needed here.

Choose the file here.

Do not create a shortcut; attach full files only.

Figure 9-3. *Find the image file you want to attach in the Insert Attachment dialog box.*

5. Locate the file.

Choose a disk drive, open folders, and finally select the file you want to attach. The file appears highlighted in the list, as shown in Figure 9-3.

6. Click the Attach button

The dialog box vanishes, and a new line in the message heading lists the attached file, as shown in Figure 9-4. The message is now ready to send.

Click here to send.

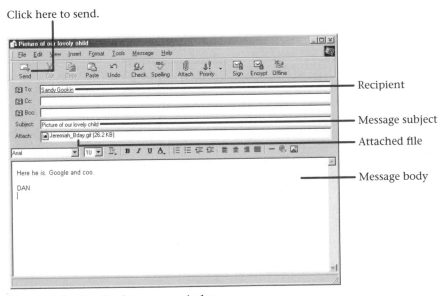

Recipient

Message subject

Attached file

Message body

Figure 9-4. *The final message window.*

In some e-mail programs, you might be able to see the image pre-viewed in the bottom of the message. Other e-mail programs may just show the file attachment as an icon at the end of the message.

7. Click the Send button to send the message.

One click and the message goes off on its merry way.

The recipient should receive the message instantly. If they're also using Outlook Express as their e-mail program, the image will be displayed right in the body of the open message, as shown in Figure 9-5.

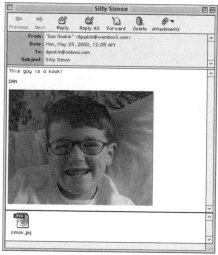

Figure 9-5. *An e-mail message with an attachment is received.*

The recipient can then save the attachment to a disk directly from the e-mail message. Simply choose the Save Attachments command from the File menu. (With some versions of Outlook Express, the Save Attachments command might be on the Message menu.) Using the dialog box that appears, choose a proper folder for the attached file, such as the My Pictures folder in Microsoft Windows Millennium.

Dealing with Problems

There's always a remote chance that the recipient might not be able to view the image you send. Some e-mail programs don't display GIF or JPEG images as Outlook Express does. In that case, you can have your friend use his or her Web browser to view the image. In addition, some e-mail programs, particularly Web-based e-mail programs, might not be able to receive the image at all. In those cases, the recipient will just have to use some other e-mail account to receive the image.

These are just general problems; any other problems you may have will be specific to the recipient. For example, there may be a rare circumstance where the recipient's computer might not be able to display a GIF image. But as long as you format and save the image as described in this chapter, you shouldn't have any problems.

Sending Images to the Web

The same formatting and saving rules for e-mail also apply to the Word Wide Web. Unfortunately, posting an image on a Web page isn't an easy list of steps that I can cover in a few pages. First you need to have "Web space" on the Internet and then some type of HTML editor to compose and create the Web page. Then after the Web pages are created, they must be uploaded, or sent, to the Internet using something called FTP.

Already in just one short paragraph I've mentioned several things that require further explanation. Egads! Web publishing isn't something that can be explained in a tiny space. You should get a good book on the subject, or at least a decent piece of software that lets you easily construct a Web page. But when you're ready, at least you'll know how to format the images properly!

Task List

1. Save an image in both GIF and JPEG format.

Scan in an image, or use a digital camera to acquire a new image, and then save it twice: once as a GIF and again as a JPEG. View the images side by side to compare their differences. If possible, try this task again using line art. Also, try saving the JPEG image at different quality levels to see how they affect the image's appearance.

2. E-mail an image to a friend.

Scan in an image, or use your digital camera, and save that image to disk. Use your e-mail program to create a new message, and attach the image to that message. Be sure to have the recipient respond and let you know that he or she got the image.

Appendix A

Questions and Answers

Q. Is there any way to take a black-and-white picture with a digital camera?

A. It really depends on the camera. Some cameras have special grayscale modes you can activate using a menu or a combination of buttons. But even if your original image was taken in color, remember that most photo-editing programs have the ability to remove color from an image and render it in grayscale. So the image can always end up in black-and-white no matter how it starts.

Q. Can I use my scanner as a copy machine?

A. Scanners make poor copy machines. It's just too time consuming to use a scanner that way: you still have to follow all the steps of previewing, scanning, transferring, and then printing. A copy machine works instantaneously. Now some scanners are built to double as copy machines and faxes, such as the Hewlett-Packard (HP) OfficeJet line of scanner/printer/faxes. In that case, yes, the scanner can be used as a copier, but only because it was designed to be used that way.

Q. If I'm just scanning pictures to send on the Internet, shouldn't I just get a digital camera instead of a scanner?

A. Absolutely. The only time you need a scanner is when you want to create digital images of photographs you already have.

Q. Can I take a digital picture of an old photograph instead of scanning it?

A. This works somewhat, as long as you hold the camera steady and ensure that the original isn't reflecting any light. The better solution is to use a scanner, which is designed specifically for this purpose.

Q. I added text to an image and cannot edit the text. What did I do wrong?

A. Nothing. Text added to an image is not editable at all; it's like painting the text on a canvas—you cannot edit the paint. And you cannot erase the text without altering the image beneath it. The solution here is to apply text on a separate layer inside the photo-editing program. That way, if you don't like the text you've added, you can delete that layer and type new text. (Working with layers is a complex issue with all photo-editing programs. Refer to a good book on your software for a detailed explanation.)

Q. I e-mailed an image to a friend, but she cannot open it. What should I do?

A. You should always save images in the GIF or JPEG format if you plan on e-mailing them. What you probably did was save the image in the "native tongue" or TIFF format. If your friend lacks any photo-editing software, she will be unable to open and view the image. Also, by not saving the image in GIF or JPEG format, you're sending your friend a very, very large file—which is unnecessary.

Q. I saved my son's artwork in the JPEG format for e-mailing, but it looks horrid. What did I do wrong?

A. Artwork and any line drawings work best in the GIF format, which is better at displaying detail than JPEG format.

Q. So what is JPEG format good for?

A. JPEG format best displays continuous tone images, such as photographs of people or landscapes or anything that's colorful.

Q. I have a question about digital imaging that's not covered in this book? Can I e-mail you a question?

A. Sure! I'm glad to support my books and will answer any question you have related to this topic that should be covered in this book. Feel free to e-mail me at *dangookin@wambooli.com*. Please be aware that I reserve the right to limit my answers to topics directly related to this book. But I do answer all my e-mail. It's my policy!

Appendix B

Popular Graphics File Types

Format	Description/Best Use
BMP	The Microsoft Windows/IBM OS/2 "bitmap" graphics file. The native format for the Paint program in Windows.
	Wallpaper in Windows. This format's files are too large for anything else.
EPS	Encapsulated PostScript, a common graphics file format for exchanging information between EPS-aware applications.
	For EPS-aware programs or printers.
GIF	The Graphics Interchange Format, owned by CompuServe but available for displaying images on the World Wide Web.
	Web images, especially detailed images
JPEG/JPG	The Joint Photographic Experts Group committee's image compression file format.
	"Real world" images for the Internet.
PDF	The Portable Document Format used by Adobe Acrobat software.
	For exchanging files with other Acrobat users.
PhotoDeluxe	The format used by Adobe PhotoDeluxe.
	PhotoDeluxe's native format.
Photoshop	The format used by Adobe Photoshop. Other programs might also be able to save and read this type of popular image format.
	Photoshop's native format.
PICT	A common format used on Macintosh computers, though not a good format for exchanging files.
	Don't use—use TIFF instead.
TIFF	The Tagged Image File Format, the most common high-resolution format for exchanging graphics files between programs.
	For sharing high-quality images between applications.

Index

Italicized page references indicate figures or tables.

Special Characters

Proof of Purchase

0-7356-1012-6

Do not send this card with your registration.
Use this card as proof of purchase if participating in a promotion or
rebate offer on *Digital Scanning and Photography*. Card must be used in conjunction with
other proof(s) of payment such as your dated sales receipt—see offer details.

Digital Scanning and Photography

_____

WHERE DID YOU PURCHASE THIS PRODUCT?

_____

CUSTOMER NAME

mspress.microsoft.com

Microsoft Press, PO Box 97017, Redmond, WA 98073-9830

OWNER REGISTRATION CARD   *Register Today!*   0-7356-1012-6

Return the bottom portion of this card to register today.

Digital Scanning and Photography

_____   _____   _____

FIRST NAME   **MIDDLE INITIAL**   **LAST NAME**

_____

INSTITUTION OR COMPANY NAME

_____

ADDRESS

_____

_____   _____   _____

CITY   **STATE**   **ZIP**

                                        (   )
_____   _____

E-MAIL ADDRESS   **PHONE NUMBER**

U.S. and Canada addresses only. Fill in information above and mail postage-free.
Please mail only the bottom half of this page.

For information about Microsoft Press® products, visit our Web site at **mspress.microsoft.com**

Microsoft®

BUSINESS REPLY MAIL
FIRST-CLASS MAIL   PERMIT NO. 108   REDMOND WA

POSTAGE WILL BE PAID BY ADDRESSEE

MICROSOFT PRESS
PO BOX 97017
REDMOND, WA 98073-9830

NO POSTAGE
NECESSARY
IF MAILED
IN THE
UNITED STATES